Change Your Standpoint
Change Your World

Change Your Standpoint
Change Your World

Kenneth George Mills

Sun-Scape Publications
Stamford • Toronto

Mr. Coleman Barks has generously given permission to use extended quotations
from copyrighted works: *The Essential Rumi,* translated by Coleman Barks with
John Moyne (San Francisco: Harper San Francisco, 1995); and *Say I Am You:
Poetry Interspersed with Stories of Rumi and Shams,* translated by John Moyne
and Coleman Barks (Athens, Georgia: Maypop, 1994).

Canadian Cataloguing in Publication Data

Mills, Kenneth G., 1923 -
    Change your standpoint, change your world

ISBN 0-919842-21-6
1. Self-realization.   2. Spiritual life.   I. Title.

BF637.S4M55 1996   158' .1   C96-931221-0

Sun-Scape Publications
A Division of Sun-Scape Enterprises Limited
1-800-437-1454
e-mail: 74601.2021@compuserve.com
WWW: http://www.sun-scape.com/

65 High Ridge Road, Suite 103
Stamford, Connecticut 06905, USA
Tel. & Fax (203) 838-3775

P.O. Box 793, Station "F"
Toronto, Ontario M4Y 2N7, Canada
Tel. (905) 470-8634. Fax (905) 470-1632

Photo credits: back cover – Neal Dahill
                inside photo – Pier Paolo Alberghini
Design: Megan MacQueen, Graphic-Painting-Grids

Printed in the United States of America

Contents

About the Author

Kenneth George Mills
Philosopher, Poet, Artist, Musician, Designer

"This is not a teaching; it is a force-field of Realignment.
This Work is the realignment of thought-structures to
conform with the chosen, unlimited Intention. If you
choose to be unreal, you will have as much strength to
be unreal and desperate as you will have choosing
the Real and being unlimited and satisfied!"

The boundless energy, innovation, and love that character-
ize the multi-faceted creative expression of Kenneth George
Mills have come forth from his unswerving fidelity to a
vow he made within himself: *"May the words of my mouth
and the meditations of my heart be acceptable in the sight
of the One altogether lovely. I will speak of my realizations
if I am asked directly and otherwise I will appear to speak
as everyone else."* Very soon after he made this vow, people
began seeking him out to ask about their deepest questions
and concerns. Ultimately, the questioning became so fre-
quent and the numbers so many that he turned to public
lecturing to accommodate this demand. Since 1968, he has
given over 30,000 hours of spontaneous metaphysical-
philosophical lectures, called *Unfoldments.*™

Intuitively, Mr. Mills turned from a successful career as
a concert pianist to this broader vocation and has been speaking with people from every walk of life, including spiritual
leaders, heads of state, performing artists, composers, international pacesetters and decision-makers. He offers public
lectures and Wordshops as well as private consultations,
explicating the profound yet practical Principle: *"I and my
Father is One, now and not shall be! Consciousness is*

fundamental, and what you are conscious of as Principle will constitute your Real experience as Conscious-Awareness, appearing manifested as a result of the Real."

His many thousands of hours of extemporaneous lectures form one of the largest private libraries ever to have been recorded and transcribed. A collection of lectures and poems has been extracted from these archives for the publication of books and spoken-word cassettes. Often, much to the surprise of Mr. Mills and the delight of his listeners, his speaking will take the form of poetry. Some 3,000 poems have been transcribed, and many of these have been gathered into four published volumes.

"The purpose of Music is to reveal to man his innate at-Onement with a harmonic State of Being."

Born in St. Stephen, New Brunswick, Kenneth Mills studied piano for 25 years and made his formal concert debut at Toronto's Eaton Auditorium in 1952. One newspaper critic acclaimed, "The whole world of glorious music is wide open to Kenneth Mills of the Maritimes." He was also recognized as one of Canada's foremost piano teachers and adjudicators.

The inception of the vocal ensemble The Star-Scape Singers, founded by Mr. Mills in 1976, heralded his discovery of a new keyboard on which to play. *"My great interest in tonal palettes was an impetus to exploring the sphere of voices set free."* This exploration resulted in the creation of a unique group of vocal artists whom critics have called "lyric pioneers in sound for the 21st century." Christopher Dedrick, James Roedl, and other well-known composers inspired by Mr. Mills' poetry, approached him with their musical settings, asking for his guidance and interpretation. He sculpted and refined their offerings, thereby co-composing over 150 original choral works, many of which are recorded on CD and cassette.

Maestro Mills and The Star-Scape Singers have performed seven times at Carnegie Hall in New York City, and their six extensive Eastern and Western European concert tours included performances at celebrated halls in Paris, Munich, Vienna, Moscow, Leningrad, Warsaw, Frankfurt and Amsterdam. They have been invited as guest artists to participate in major international festivals in Switzerland, Ireland, France, Poland, Czechoslovakia, Russia, and the Baltic Republics. Wherever they have traveled, the Singers and their conductor have served as a powerful force for world harmony and unity.

"You are to play great parts. How can you play a great part and have such small concepts about your Self?"

In the midst of one man's dramatic considerations was a scenario conceived of dramatizing the spontaneous monologue given by Kenneth Mills and making it a polyphonic experience presented to him by a group of actors at a Christmas party. It was so well received that Mr. Mills sponsored the troupe, now known as the EarthStage Actors. Since 1989, they have been dedicated to presenting his poetry and prose in a dramatic form which reviewers have called a "theater of philosophy" and "modern-day Shakespeare."

EarthStage's programs are uniquely inspired as the actors have the rare privilege of being directed by the author himself in discovering and expressing the many levels of meaning hidden within the scripts. He works in great detail with each actor's voice, showing that the accurate intoning of sound can create for the listener a doorway to a new perspective on these most provocative, philosophical ideas.

The EarthStage Actors have performed on stage and over radio broadcast throughout North America.

"Beauty may be present,
but without Elegance
there is no aroma."

Kenneth Mills' wonder and appreciation of universal beauty and order have also found expression through his designs. He has created two lines of haute couture women's evening wear, marketed as *Moulins Originale,* which accentuate the elegance and regality of the feminine. Exquisite fabrics and jewel-like colors reflect his characteristic daring and joie de vivre. These fashions were shown in a spectacular gala presentation at the Ed Sullivan Theater, New York City, in 1993. It combined, for the first time, a live fashion show with the phenomenon of High-Definition television in portraying an evening of unique beauty which was entitled the "Integrity of Elegance." He has also designed for his *Kg Collections* label a superbly versatile line of ready-to-wear fashion for businesswomen.

In addition to his women's and men's fashions, the flow of his creative inspiration has extended into unique designs for homes, gardens, furniture, jewelry and fragrances. He has also consulted with architects on designs for arts and cultural centers, concert halls, and communities.

"Great art never leaves you . . where it finds you.
Great art reveals what is not seen by giving you
a painting to look at while the work
of the Real art is seen where
it is not painted."

Kenneth Mills' visual art arose spontaneously early in 1993, to his own amazement and that of those around him. The sudden prompting to paint resulted in a prolific production of some 150 canvasses in the following two years. One might well say that the artist is Self taught, as the power to his brush has brought forth an unprecedented expression, blossoming as flowers, landscapes and portraits.

In March 1995, a selection of these paintings was displayed at the international ArtExpo '95 at the Jacob Javits Center in New York City. Mr. Mills' main medium is acrylics, although he is also exploring other artistic media.

▼ ▼ ▼

In 1996, PRIME Mentors of Canada (PMC) for the Development of Creative Potential selected Kenneth Mills to be the 1997 Honorary PRIME Mentor.

June 13, 1996

Dear Mr. Mills:

It is my great pleasure and privilege to inform you that the PRIME Mentors of Canada (PMC) has selected you to be the 1997 Honorary PRIME Mentor for being an exemplary mentor to many appreciative and devoted protégés and for serving as a role model par excellence whom society could look up to for inspiration and guidance.

Conchita Tan-Willman, Ph.D.
Founder/President - PRIME Mentors of Canada

Foreword

Something beckoned you to pick up this book and open its pages. Take a moment and consider why you were thus prompted. Did the enticement appear external, perhaps something intriguing about the title or the colors of the cover? Or could it be that, as Kenneth George Mills says in the first chapter, "Choice Words":

> You have come out from the audience and have responded to an inner demand which has appeared perhaps as an invitation; it has appeared perhaps as a hope; or it could have appeared as an opportunity (or as a curiosity) to sit for a moment and to consider your impersonal nature and your great offering — through the perception of the course of Truth that is before you . . .

If there is a response or a recognition, a desire for change or for a more comprehensive viewpoint, you would do well to first take stock of where you think you are right now. What do you feel is your purpose, your modus operandi? What are your hopes and expectations? Make note in some fixed manner that can be observed later, because once you have devoted your attention to this "manual of the art of Being," you will never be the same!

Why? You are about to read several scores from what could be termed "the Symphony of Soul," and although you may not be able to hear its totality, you will know that you have a part to play in the orchestra of Light by the very nature of your inner response to the chordal structure. When a note is sounded, any opened strings pitched in accord begin to vibrate in harmonic agreement. As you feel these harmonic vibrations, you will see how you have been granted an opportunity to *Change Your Standpoint ~ Change Your World*.

But beware! You will have given up your life of normality. You will have surrendered your "right" to remain a passenger on the train of chance, a wanderer without a home, a victim without a cause. You will have been "found out," identified — not by some external agent but *as* the most irreconcilable Force known to man: the Self. For as Kenneth Mills says, "You cannot entertain a divine Idea and not have a corresponding identity!"

The text of his remarkable tonal weavings will reveal how you are irrevocably encompassed by destiny, firmly seated in the chair of responsibility, and in possession of all the talents and merits, the tools and opportunities to BE everything that you already are in the perfect archetypal sense of Conscious-Being.

If you picked up this book merely out of curiosity, or doubting that its title bears a possibility, then put it back before you are committed! Do not venture further if you are satisfied with yourself as you think you are, if you are content with the appearance of the world, if you have no thirst for meaning — or if you do not believe in miracles!

Kenneth Mills welcomes the "few who perceive the adventure of appearing as the discoverers of a lost continent termed 'the Self'" and provides road maps for a most exciting venture into a realm where the course is always new. Let the intellect play second fiddle, for the outpourings of this modern-day Sage are as non-linear as they are intuitive, as insightful as they are challenging to "mortal mind." Subdue the temptation to rationalize, open your ears and heart, and read as if you were listening to a symphony. It has been said by Kenneth Mills that *analysis never heals;* also remember that analysis is always after the fact, and the real joy of music comes when you allow limited mind-concepts to bow to the naturally unfolding, harmonic pattern.

The lectures constantly pour forth, un-thought, un-rehearsed or pre-meditated, and speak to the conditions of those who have asked or called to hear. They are an interesting phenomenon and are simply called spontaneous *Unfoldments.*™ The talks are usually given in a formal setting to varied audiences including professionals from almost every field: businessmen, diplomats, doctors, lawyers, designers, artists, musicians, students, teachers, homemakers, and hard workers. All have "tuned in" to his presence through direct or indirect contact — such as you have in picking up one of his many publications — and have come, asking to hear him speak about key life features of which they may not even be aware.

The answers, miraculously and uniquely sounded by the Speaker, are always profound, provocative (sometimes challenging), and pertinent unto each and every listener because the Truths which Kenneth Mills utters are fundamentals of the universe and are practically evidenced in the undeviating example of his life, founded on the Principle which he has given as "I and my Father *is* One, now and not shall be." In your reading (best done aloud), these various aspects of divine Mind will undoubtedly bear relevance to you, too, but you should also know that meeting this master musician-magician-composer, this world-server, will provide a more direct and rewarding communication of the Word than does its written symbol.

Kenneth Mills' message awakens and re-aligns us to our highest purpose and can enable us to experience the gratitude and joy of moving in accord with the opportunity to:

> . . . See your place in stifling the suggestions of time and offering a way for this world and the people therein to achieve once again that State that is termed harmonic and rhythmic and in keeping with that known as Heaven here and now.

The doors are open, the orchestra tuned, the conductor raising his baton. Claim your place and prepare to experience how the limits of time and space are swallowed up in the Music of the Spheres.

Neal Dahill

Editor's Notes

Kenneth Mills uses the words "you," "me," "I," and "I AM" in a very specific sense. The "you" and the "me," especially when stressed, refer to the imaginary entities that we have created in our minds and claimed to be the identity of both ourselves and others. The "you" and the "me" represent the state of thought that believes itself to be embodied physically and thus part and parcel of a material world. It is our conceptual identity; it is a limited, corporeal self-image that we have been educated to construct on the premise of duality and materiality. In short, it is the human personality that parades one way one minute and another way the next.

The "I AM" is the infinite, the eternal, and the unchanging. The I or the I AM is our true Identity. The I AM is what we really are. It is beyond any thought that can be identified with the finite. It is not a conceptual identity, for it cannot be conceived, yet it is the Light to all conception. The I AM is synonymous with other terms appearing in the text: Consciousness, the Source, the Self, Christ, Truth, Life, Love, the Light, That which IS. Yet, we cannot think in terms of being That personally, because this would impose a limit on the I AM, which is limitless.

The use of "We," when capitalized, is explained by Mr. Mills:

> "We" always points to the all-inclusive nature used by royalty and is always considered a grace, for it is a divine all-inclusiveness, thus capitalized and set apart in the Lectures, pointing to the impersonal Nature and its all-encompassing activity.

Preface

May the contents of this book be an answer to the whys and why-nots in a world that is verging on the giddiness that erupts on the edge of choice. The next millennium which is being so dreamed will be far from the fulfilling of an emancipated state, when those viewing it are caught in the realm of delusion.

May you find that to change your world rests with you! The world is not a problem; the problem is the refusal to make your intention golden and see the world as it *really* IS.

K. G. Mills
July 9, 1996

To enjoy its Truth, read it out loud and hear the inner Voice. The power of the sounded Word will enthuse an acknowledged knowing within your Being and you will be surprised and smile at the simplicity of the Light and Love expressed as Kenneth Mills.

– Rolland G. Smith
T.V. Anchorman

Chapter I

Choice Words

gratitude

Heaven here-now

Identity

Word

Choice Words

This evening we are here in a country home, and the fire is blazing away and the hearth is very warm, and it does warm the cockles of the heart to know that there are a few who perceive the adventure of appearing as the discoverers of a lost continent termed "the Self." Never has the world needed such Light to be shed upon the course of events as it is now perceived in the annals of historical suggestion.

The apparent need for the freedom from an alleged false identity will be found to be of great, great importance because, until you shed the skin of belief, you can never experience that pulsation of Being that allows you a prerogative of divinity. You have come out from the audience and have responded to an inner demand which has appeared perhaps as an invitation; it has appeared perhaps as a hope; or it could have appeared as an opportunity (or as a curiosity) to sit for a moment and to consider your impersonal nature and your great offering — through the perception of the course of Truth that is before you but does not *lie* before you. It establishes the direct approach to the magic of giving the world back to the arms of Love.

For all those seen and unseen, as we sometimes say, gratitude is expressed for your presence, because you could not possibly be here if some aspect of you did not deem it essential. Your querulous mind filled with suggestions and its floppy-disk characteristics would never have gotten you to the steps of this abode had there not been a power present that caused each footstep to be taken as if imprinted into the accuracy of your nature for the expedient release from a false, conjured concept about yourself. There is no time at our disposal. To think that there *is* is only a sedated consideration that time is involved with your releasement from a false identity!

People often say, "How is a Teaching like this practical?" As you all know, being practical, you find yourselves here. It is practical to article for the Law regardless of your degree in the judicial system, for to-day it is essential that there be those who are capable of sounding a tone, or eliciting one from someone, that will alert you to the inherent factor within your Self that causes you to respond to the magic and wonder of an authentic State that allows the illusion to appear and yet to be known as *I* IS.

You cannot entertain what is termed a divine Idea and not have a corresponding identity. That is the practicality of what is termed "the Absolute" or "the Path of the Uncontradictable" or "the ninth Yoga Path," as I have been told. I just use these paths to try to make you feel more at home. I know nothing about them. You in your learned state perhaps know far more about them than I do. I am just a candy-maker's son who knew what it was to have a sweet father and a sweet mother, and who knew the meaning of keeping one's word.

To-day, the keeping of words is not very sacred. People use them as if they were running from a tap in the kitchen and try to wash off the dishes of their thought, but as you know, you have to use soap to get them clean! There is nothing more readily at hand to erase the film from your experience than the All. Blue Cheer is available and so is Tide. The tide is always coming-in and going-out.

If you have sight, do claim the All and see how the blind are healed, the deaf hear, the mute is removed from the strings of your Heart, and you start once again responding with the accuracy of authenticity to those strings that are geared to what is termed the seven-stringed lyre accompanying such words as "I love wondrous Light!"

These few words may appear to be far sent but they do appear in the tonality of my appearance, for you are present. If you were not present, no Word like this would be heard. Since you *are* present and the Word is heard, we know then, within the fabric of our knowingness, that there is not a word that comes from the lyre of the Heart and proceeds into the vestibule of your presence that does not bear with it the auditory response to the sound, so penetrating the veil of suggestions that you respond with the perception of absolute value, as you see your place in stifling the suggestions of time and offering a way for this world and the people therein to achieve once again that State that is termed harmonic and rhythmic and in keeping with that known as Heaven here and now.

It is not some place that you are going to go to. If you think it is, it is hell! When you live knowing that I AM the Force to your presence, then you know that the comfort comes, for you do not have to declare yourself to be present because you are so assured of the omnipresence and the omni-action of that constant Presence known as I AM that allows your pseudonym to be utilized and dropped at will as you engage once again the rhythmic dance from sense to Soul.

These few words preface this meeting in somewhat the staid offering of choice words, for they do come forth involuntarily. They are said for you who are to hear, and having ears, I pray you hear.

▼

Chapter II

An Epiphany of Wonder

chaos

male/female

past/present/future

Adam/Eve

intention

Word/oral tradition

Oneness

An Epiphany of Wonder

We have been considering in great depth from a plane of observation the objective drama that is being enacted upon this stage. The variegated pattern is observed, the characteristics are observed, and the attraction is observed, without any involvement, from the standpoint of an observer. This information is being dropped onto your plate-of-attention in order for you to partake of an essential approach to the chaos which surrounds the people on this plane.

As the Ancients called forth those who could perceive — as the Elders of Moses, the seventy Silent Ones, were called forth in order to hold a point of concentrated intention in order to stabilize a divine intention — so are you called as part of the Selected Force in order to help stabilize without emotion the Force that is likened unto a transformation. It is known that the masculine force is termed "fire," and the feminine force is termed "passive." It is a concern, a cool concern for those who hear these words, to consider what is moving within them as they partake of this time-space continuum and its scenario.

Some have offered that the windows of gigantic possibilities are open for just a few short years, and yet the people are dismayed, for they run amok in the objective realm. For those who participate, a requirement is to **perceive within yourself the purity of the intention.** Unless your intention is pure, the results in your experience are questionable. If the intention is pure, it bears the enhancement of the Invisible, for it gives confidence, to those confronting chaos, of the only authentic State.

If you perceive the chaos, it is because you are not in it; if your thought associates with the chaos, you are in it! If your thought commiserates with the chaos, you enhance the chaos. If in your witnessing you are holding the point of the observer, then you are capable of perceiving the next move, which may not bear a recognizable acceptance among those disturbed in the mentality, for logic and reasoning are great friends of the sophist; they are so clever in their argumentation and in their augmentation of partials in order to appear erudite and hopefully remain undetected as superficial!

Anything that is superficial lacks substance! Why should you expect the world, the stage, to be in any other condition than it is if it were not for a salient feature of your observation? If you can *see* the lack of rhythm, the lack of harmony, the *lack,* then you know there is something allowing the "you" to perceive. *You do not need to be in it if you will adopt and adapt to the frequency of the Invisible!*

Why do we have such confidence in harmony, in rhythm, in melody? We have confidence in the harmony because the very basis of perception of the objective world or the very perception of another or the very perception of a flower is all possible because of this connection that exists in the silence of Being. It states that a component of Principle is that a divine Idea has a corresponding identity, so that identity has a harmony which is part of the womb of ideation. It has a rhythm as part of that contraction of propelling possibilities, and when heard interiorly has a melody without words! Thus we have a firm foundation on which even the neophyte has an access to confidence.

In this professed intention of seeking the invisible, the immutable, and the indivisible Oneness of Being, we know that we are at that point of wonder when we can see not God *in matter* but God appearing in such a way, the Source appearing in such a way, that even in the world of chaos the Source is known to exist, either there would be no hope of achieving peace and a resolution of conflict in any sphere of the world.

This formality is being evidenced in answer to the unspoken demand of conviction. If the seeker is not *convinced* of his temporal nature (which he must be as he sees it changing), then he is at a loss to know what to do about chaos. When the seeker *is* convinced that there is a Source of his beingness, then he adopts even such a myth as Adam and Eve and hopes for a genesis of significance!

How can you expect a fulfillment, an epiphany of wonder, to happen if you are looking and thinking through the thought-forms that have accumulated? They have accumulated and are worthless if they do not conform to a standard, and *that standard is one of perfection.* This perfection is not considered obtainable in the flesh. We know that in our attempt at perfection we see it is not what we think it is. Perfection has as a component a clear intention and a flexibility component that allows thoughts to be dropped and the sail of infinite possibilities to be filled with the omnipotent breath of rapture.

Why do we say "rapture"? Because it is a feeling of buoyancy becoming a Conscious-Awareness-Body. The only body that bears weight is "you" and the only body that seems to cognize other bodies bearing the same heaviness is all found in the realm of "you" — not that we expect those bodies to don wings! No "you" can don wings. It usually has horns, for "you" is seldom other than obstinate and willful in maintaining what you have accumulated in . . knowledge?

If you cannot walk and bear a uniqueness and an ability to "rap" with the unheard rhythmic pattern of the Uncontradictable, you are in the arena where you must find a way to discipline the thought to conform to the standard of excellence, which means it transcends anything that you have considered possible. *Excellence is the name given to something that you have not considered possible.* You can see how it has been weakened by saying, "Oh, that was excellent." As soon as excellence becomes a past condition, it no longer comes from a constant Source.

> **Excellence is really the involuntary excelling**
> **in the creative artistry of God-Being,**
> **involuntarily manifested to satisfy the need**
> **of those who ask for food!**

We consider the formations of our time and how to juggle the observed, the mixture, the males and the females, to put it simply. It shows you how complex this type of simplicity is! The simplicity I speak of does not have anything to do with this complexity, because the simplicity that *IS* perceives the complexity that *isn't* as simply solved in perceiving the underlying and overlying unity.

This is why the oral tradition is so sacred. If the Word bears an inseminating force, it is because God-Man equals male-female — One. It is stated that God made man; He created man; male-female created He them.

Adam and Eve are not the beginning of your race! They have been the beginning of your supposition that you are "this." Adam and Eve in the garden were not male and female in form. Adam and Eve were the male and female principle and, when not understood, or concealed from the uninitiated, were represented as men and women. The fruit, the apple, was forbidden, because if you took of the fruit you pierced the skin of the suggestion and you perceived that you were not divided; but misinterpretation has said that you were divided and therefore not satisfied.

When this is perceived clearly, you have to pinch yourself ("pinch-me-tight"[1]) because "you" start to fade out in the ebullience of the Conscious-Awareness experience. You

---

1. Reference is being made to a children's rhyme.

have to "pinch-me-tight" to be sure that "this" still remains able to observe and appear to be in what is observed, never found as a thing but as a force that is termed "the magic to the wonder of encounter."

The reason the oral tradition is so significant is because it can do one of two things: It can cause you, on the lowest level, to remember; it can cause you, on the higher level, to listen. On the lower level you can be called to remember, to remember what was possible within the cache of inherited Light-credits that you have (but have forgotten that you have), and then to be led to the point where, upon considering these, you may start to *listen.*

Few hear because few remember.

This is why you study to find yourself approved. You study to find yourself approved as a neophyte by offering your paragraphs to the elders for comments. When you find yourself approved you are not known to be approved within yourself; you feel the buoyancy of an elder's adjudication, and this points to the less dense thought-form holding you in bondage to a knowledgeable realm.

If the future depended upon your knowledge of what to do with it, it would be better to go into the Rockies, into the Pyrenees, or into the Ural Mountains, or to disappear! There is nothing that you can do from the standpoint of person to remove the superficial action of those who have failed to perceive that they bear false masks called persons, personality and its complexes. *Personality complexes are the result of interior, conflicting thought-patterns that have lost their moorings in Principle or stabilized fact.*

If this statement finds acceptance within you, it points to the fact that you are more than what appears as the one hearing this. *Why do you go on perpetuating the density of supposition when your awareness could bear the luminosity of another Presence and another kingdom?*

If you are to remove the bushel basket from over your head, let the head go with it! We know that was the reason Victory was winged, because the head went to the solar Heart and God gave wings to the form. In other words, it became capable of transcendent flight. Winged Victory is the symbol of accomplishment.[2] Victory can never be gained by arming many for a foray without giving the many the force of one to one. What does one to one mean? The force of one to one is One, perhaps to the second power. What is the second power? Hearing. W*hen man has achieved One, he bears the ability to indite.*

Last evening we were speaking in the most wonder-filled way of the situation which appears, the situation of contradictions, and the Way of pristine splendor. There was a considerable joy at the presence of such intention and attention that much could happen in the way of interior revelation. One of the key features that was pointed out was the need to observe your language. It may be of interest to you to perceive in all these typed pages if "I" has been used.

It is essential to rescind the inclination to try to invoke force by using "I." You think the "I" is a magic power in the mind of a person. It is not! The magic of *I* is not other than in a fount of Sound.

The Way is marked with authenticity when the participant, "you," experiences, as a natural function of the day, the creative action commensurate with the unified force of a divine concept: the unity of male-female. It is such a gigantic concept to the mind that thinks dualistically. It is such a simple statement, but if you will note, the tendency of the object that appears to talk, to walk, and sometimes to think, is always to associate with its members of like-kind in order to bear force of conviction. This is why the Selected are called. *If the mass of time is mesmerized in the pattern and propaganda of division, the Select Force knows the unitary Principle of universal significance, giving the world-stage*

---

2. "Winged Victory" is the name of a statue in the Louvre in Paris.

back to the umbrella of Love's embrace so that it can come under the solar embrace of a wonder.

Some talk of the future as a New Age dawning and talk about the Aquarian Age. These are like chapter headings or selections on a program of entertainment for the mesmerized. If you remember, do so. The past is nothing but a figment of imagination. Why do you say "imagination"? Because you have thoughts that go with it. Imagination always has thoughts that go with it. If thoughts go with the past, why do you not let them? The future comes with a thought. Why? *The future is the name given to the bifurcated present. This is why it is such a point to perceive when thought is stilled, I AM.*

A thought declares something-or-other. It is a thought that declares a beginning and an end. But if there is one divine Conscious-Awareness-Thought, it has no beginning or end! This is the only time that "thought" can be capitalized, because the one divine Thought is without beginning or end. It is sometimes called Source, sometimes called Self, sometimes called God, and sometimes called the Word; in other words, many of them — until you perceive that words lead you to where there are not any. **The Word unuttered is like a lightning bolt and uttered is like the thunder that follows to the densities below.**

If you are a selected force, then you must have the ability to be the custodians of a knowingness that allows you to penetrate the suggestion of chaos and perceive it as nothing but an act to seduce you into a belief system of deterioration. All the bonfires, all the wars, all the upsets in so many nations in the world are all vehicles or means of taking your attention. If you give them your attention, you give them your power, unless you can observe them without involvement but with *compassion.*

Compassion is not emotion. Compassion is the power of restoring involuntarily by Presence.

You do not say someone is not suffering. You take care of the suffering, but **never forsake your God-Being and chase the shadow!** You never try to restore order unless you are asked to restore it, verbally. You are the order to the disorder, either you could not have cognized the disorder. If another recognizes the order, it is because you are ordered and he is ordered and has asked for order in his disordered state! When a person asks for order to a disordered state, he often goes to a psychologist or a psychiatrist in order to find order for his disordered state, seldom asking if the practitioner is ordered and capable of ordering *his* disordered state! [laughter]

It seems so simple to retrieve or make-up histories to give you confidence that you lived before and had ancestors. What is the point of ancestors if they are gone? Are they waiting for you? Is that the value of an ancestor? The value of an ancestor is that it is the backdrop for present freedom from a belief system to be enacted! *It does not take time to think right. It takes willingness and the energy to change!* When you have the energy to change, you say you are *charged,* not like a battery that has to be plugged in after so many hours of usage. Then you will have an ancestry: the charging business! [laughter]

You do not want that type of pact with the past. Your present is so fecund with possibilities if you would put a value on the words that you speak, on your actions that evidence creativity. Remember, *it is the male principle that is creative; it is the female that is passive. How many males appear passive? How many males appear creative? How many females appear passive? How many females appear creative?* You cannot get an answer from that realm. All you can get from that realm is heat of argumentation! You are cool when you see where people are in their remembering. *They must remember that they of themselves can do nothing.* They could not make even the lily of the field or the grass of the lawn or cause a hair follicle to dance, if it were not for the wonder of a bridge between the Invisible and the visible.

This is why you can have such confidence because you are told that *I* will never leave you comfortless. This is how it is perceived that the statement "Comfort ye my people" can be fulfilled. They are permitted to see, if they so wish to see, the bridge between the invisible and the visible, the infinite and the finite, and the unification of the male-female — One! Even that statement could not have been made if the Word were not One before it appeared divided as male-female. The sound "male-female" is still sound, but **do you remember that *"you"* associated with division?** *I* **associates with unity, the Oneness of creative expression.**

The Absolute seems so sterile until you start to *perceive*. Then there is no contradiction; there is only the Diction. "Contra" is "against," and that is what those who take bits and pieces and are not prepared do to an outpouring as a result of request.

Remember? *Re*quest, *re*visit, *re*locate, *re*spond, *re*-assemble, *re*-member. If you appear to be membered you will assemble, for there is but one divine attraction and that is Love. It is Love that is forever present, but misunderstood is considered an emotion. Thus, an attempt at unity, appearing as marriage, is frequently annulled or brought to an end. There was no victory in experiencing unity. You cannot experience unity from the standpoint of bringing two forms together, unless you are so attained that you appear like light electrical bodies, penetrating and interpenetrating the spheres of even the thought-realm and the molecular realm of your supposition. Then you are calling upon such a state of affairs that no one can say what shall be or what shall not be.

There is no future. That is on your program as part of your act to be fulfilled as a present creative act. Those who witness it to-morrow will say it was in the future that it happened, and you will say, "That is how you saw my present moment due to your belief in a serial of time." My present moment is a victory, for how can *I* be present and still have come from a timeless, zoneless place?

Light is static until it strikes the responsive nature of cognition. Then hearing becomes the higher and remembering the lower. Both are embraced in the natural beneficence of the divine authority.

The monarchy represents such an incredible ideal, and people have forgotten what it represents because the powers sitting on the throne may not have been schooled to represent the undivided state appearing as male-female — One.

What does it matter? A great deal, because if you can see a sage-like monarchy, then you have an example. What is an example for? To emulate. Why do you adore? In order to make yourself closer to what is adored, and as soon as you do that, you become what you thought you adored. **What you adore is all within yourself, but until you know that, it is well to adore!** A thought-filled mind will say, "You make a god out of this one or that one, and that is awful! What are you doing about those close to you? Annulling us?" "No! Seeing you as you really are, for I adore what I have found!"

What you are searching for in your *re*-quest to hear is now known never to have been lost, either I would not have spoken. **If what you request to BE had been lost, *I* would never have been found.** Is it not a miracle that in the assembly of the lost, what was lost is found — and the department (lost and found) does not even know it?! They want a label on it: "What is your name? No, there's no article here . . under that name." Why? That Name could never be lost!

The simplicity of Being is wrapped in the rhythm and the harmonic nature that is so in keeping with your heart's desires.

> **Do not lose the elegance of Being.**
> **Do not lose the wonder of a Reappearance.**
> **Do not lose the point of reassembly,**
> **and do not accept anything that is unlike**
> **the All that IS.**

Do not use "I" to give "you" importance.
If you are cognized and a re-quest is made,
it is obvious, *I* is present.
Know . . *before* . . you called,
I have answered.

HEAR that! It is the higher level.

Before . . you called.
I answered.

For you who have heard me speak of "he" and "she" and the heishe beads,[2] now you see the symbolic nature: The *he* of Adam and the *she* of Eve are worn together around the neck as an ornament of adornment. It is the he-she. The he-she has the **S** on its side; it is the symbol of the invisible breath, of the movement of the breath, and that is how it is creative and living.

This seems a dictation of import, carefully worded, worded carefully. Handle with care!

Develop the higher faculty, intuition, and *understand* "Before ye called, I answered."

If you have not the intuitive faculty, *remember:* **Before . . you called. I answered.**

This bears reference to your historical past in the legacy of Socrates, Plato, any of the greats, because any great bore the same plateau of wonder. It was on this plateau that all spoke, to those who converged on the steps of it, of the wonder, for the market-place became a place not only of selling wares but of ridding oneself of a false identity.[3]

---

2. "Heishe beads" are made by Native Americans in the Southwest.
3. "Market-place" refers to the Agora, where Socrates taught and spoke of Identity.

The point of the Selected is to stabilize the knowing fulfillment of a fulfilled *re-quest* after the fullness of correct Identity.

[Mr. Mills looks at his watch.] *I came so that there would be time no longer!* [laughter]

What is the point of believing and basing your life on a limit? If "you" are the limit, *change your identity!*

Down East they used to say when you were little, "Oh, wake-up and die right!" Are you so old that you cannot wake-up — and die immediately?! Do not allow Love as life to be other than "big as life"!

> Without Love, a mountain is a mountain,
> And with Love, a mountain is a mountain.
> Without Love, you may try to scale it.
> With Love, you may observe it and cause its
>   snow hat to melt in the solar might
> Of involuntarily beaming a wonder unto its
>   heights.

Have confidence.

> You could never have considered Source if it
>   were not available to you.
> You could never have considered Source if
>   you were not one with it, because it is
>   an original idea;
> It is your thought that gives you more than
>   one idea!

You could never have considered Love if Love were not all there is to you, allowing itself to be considered in your doubtful nature, and giving you the confidence to be its manifestation, involuntarily bestowing what is essential on the stage called "the world."

Oh, boy! Oh, girl! Be united in O! Do not go around in circles! *Find the Point and then allow your radius of activity to extend in all directions so that the circumference of your experience is blessed involuntarily by the radiation of your volcanic and fire Center. That is the only way a blaze of glory is considered commensurate with an epiphany of wonder!*

▼ ▼ ▼

Lillian L.) Mr. Mills, your words went straight to my heart, and I would like to thank you with all my heart for your wisdom knowledge.

Thank you, Lillian. We are undivided in the I-Light. In the I-Light, Love is redolent in its adaptations and bestowals. This is how the restoration of the Monarchy is achieved, by restoring it within yourself. Then if you see it outside yourself, you will know it is for *good*, for if you have succeeded in restoring it within yourself, then the mountains become hills and the rugged places plain and your cave of seclusion the busiest corner on any street in any city! **Wherever I AM is holy, for the ground of Being is forever verdant in the inner state of a permanent, constant newness and freshness.**

If there is any concern at all about your form, it is because you have failed to identify beyond the personality, the person, the mask of superficiality. Ascend unto that holy Spot beyond all time, and then you will find that you are right where others stand but you mark the Spot that is *immovable*, for from it you are radiating the wonders of a creative spirit that allows you the flexibility of being Real.

▼

Chapter III

Marked with Meaning

role/part

seeing/hearing

statesmanship

new birth

intention

radiance

Center/Origin

Marked with Meaning

I was considering this morning that the reason an entire map or the plan or the picture of a puzzle is so helpful is because it gives you an overview of the puzzle. What is the chief characteristic of any one part of a puzzle? Yes, Katrine.

> Katrine G.) A characteristic of a part of a puzzle is that it has a corresponding form to match it.

In other words, every piece is clearly defined. Every statement is clearly defined. I wanted you to perceive how it is not the size of the piece but the *definition* of the piece that constitutes the revealment of the picture. This is very important to perceive. How do you know where a piece goes? Chris.

> Christopher D.) When a piece is right, it does not have to be forced into place; it fits, snaps perfectly into place.

Perfectly into place — and every part that is fitly joined together is marked. It does not just fit, *it bears a marking*.

Each piece bears a marking. You can say, "That mark doesn't mean anything; this mark doesn't mean anything; that mark doesn't mean anything." It does not, by itself. This is the value of group action. By itself a piece does not mean anything other than *it belongs to something!* How many people have said to you, "I know you are special, you belong to something"? "What are you doing? You have had a special Teaching." You have a *marking* that means nothing and yet means something. *This* is the mark that does not have meaning by itself.

This is why it is stated, through the manifested channels of time, that *those who gather together with a defined intention are marked.*[1] What does it say? "It is by their fruits and gifts that ye shall know them." It has been stated: "Beloved son of the Light, always behold the gifts. By their gifts shall they be known unto you." That is what I was once told.

"By their gifts shall they be known unto you." It is fascinating when you stop and consider it this way. The gift of Presence is marked, but unless it is fitly joined with force to the picture, it does not bear the impact! For example, if Lucille were on her own, she could be a consultant to many businesses, but when she has the prestige and the power of a recognized international company behind her, it marks her as being part of a picture that is comprehensive. That is what the picture of the jigsaw puzzle does! *It gives you a comprehensive view.*

The purpose for which we have come together may be that, by finding the Center Piece, *your* piece starts to have meaning because you start to perceive the markings upon your Scrolls that have been indelibly etched with the purpose of your intention as an incarnate. It has absolutely nothing whatsoever to do with the position in which you find yourself to-day! It is one thing to say "I know the

---

1. "You cannot *think* intention. I AM Intention! Intention is defined motivation as creativity." — K. G. Mills

Center Piece"; it is another to be able to say "I can show it to you." If you cannot say "I can show you," all you can build is a theoretical basis of operation. This is of little value, because theory without practice allows theory to maintain a position of authority it really does not have.

The jigsaw puzzle is intriguing to the mind because they say there is the side of the brain that loves to deal with fragments and the other side that creates a picture. But there is nothing to interfere with the completion of the picture when both sides are in agreement with the fun of seeing the composite whole. It is a very different story when the "pieces" live and move and appear to have their own being!

What makes a group, what makes a corporation, what makes a nation, unsteady? The people starting to lose the definition of their parts in defining the character and the culture of the picture that that nation or place of incarnation contains. A nation loses itself and its possibilities by losing the definition of markings. The pseudo-culture of an intellectual agenda is such that it blurs the markings of the average selected force by the indoctrination of a pattern of familiarity with intellectual concepts. We feel at ease with certain prescribed forms of induction and deduction and with a certain prescribed form of dialectics, but it is extremely challenging to try to define the character of a situation from the standpoint of having a blurred outline and a blurred meaning of yourself.

Why do I suddenly personify "yourself" as a piece? Because the wholeness appears to be fractured for the parts to be played in order to perceive the undying ember of the total composite picture that is etched within the Scroll of your remembrance. Those who have tried to refute the natural inclination to incline the ear have allowed the sensorial dictatorship of the eyes to superimpose a visual adjudication. Such adjudication evaluates a situation without allowing *hearing* to be primary. It has been stated that "having ears ye hear not and eyes ye see not." It is fascinating when you consider the part you have played to this point.

It is interesting to see how few parts fit mine with definition! Why do you suppose that is, when the jigsaw puzzle is machine cut, machine defined? Yet, the jigsaw puzzle is only possible from a picture that has never been cut in any way; it has been a work of art! That work of art is a masterstroke of attainment: your legacy.

Why do you perpetuate the fallacious state of student-ship instead of **statesmanship?** The students should have graduated and statesmen should have been born. Why? *The statesman has the State of meaning marking his performance, which is essential to the elucidation of the whole!* This cannot be left up to an intellectual persuasiveness of whether or not it shall be adopted by "you." In fact, it does not want "you" at all! It wants you to appear as the State of that which is *marked with meaning* for this new birth.

It is obvious we are on the very edge of a new birth. We are birthing something new, painfully new. It is important for you to perceive the pain surrounding a new birth if you are reluctant to assume a natural rhythm. Women are trained when they are birthing to develop a natural breathing and rhythm so that the offspring will be able to come forth easily.

If the statesman of the future is cognized, he cannot be seen as one meandering and ruminating; there is no time for meandering and there is no time for fulminating over the situations of the past, which come to the front of your considerations in the pressure moments of the changed demands. *If you will notice, your inclination is always to revert to the past to support an obstinacy that appears in the present. As soon as you activate that, you blur the precision of your marking.*

Where do you usually work out a jigsaw puzzle? On a flat surface. Everything happens initially with your jigsaw puzzle on a flat surface with all the parts strewn on it, with no indication of where any part belongs. This is exactly what happens in this situation. When there were several hundred people present, there were several hundred parts, but as people perceived their markings and saw where they belonged, they tried to blur their definition so that they would have leeway. If you are selected to be present, as you are and have been (even the people who are not here are still here!), you are in the Conscious-Awareness-pattern of the totality. That is why those who have left can never be excluded; no matter what they say about me or you, they can never be excluded from the face of the Plan.

Everyone in the entire world, bearing an inheritance similar to the one etched in the pattern of a Promise, bears within himself an ember of totality that is known to exist, but *it is not found anywhere within his intellectual achievement.* It is not part of the paraphernalia of the mind! It is part of the enhancement that comes with that portion of Being that bears with it the impinging force of non-matter. [pause] That is termed "knowing there is something beyond your three-dimensional experience." It is enhanced by the force of an unconfined conception. This demands a finely pitched sensitivity to the Soul! *It is the most questionable aspect of an alien to this planet.*

We say there are the aboriginals. We say that because we know there is an ember of creativity and it must have a corresponding identity. We do not know what comes *after* us. We *do* know that what comes *before* us must be something that we are not, something that was the original. The aboriginals are those whom we do not understand because we have lost the wonder of Origin. Losing the wonder of Origin is losing the wonder that allows what appears as our environment in a three-dimensional world to talk.

If the environment does not talk to you and tell you of your Origin, it is because you have distanced yourselves from the instant when a Star broke the horizon of the mind and caused a rift in the mentality. That is all this *Unfoldment*™ has ever done — caused a rift in your mentality — because you have taken the first part of the word "mentality" and made yourself "men" of that condition. You did not know what to call the other part. It was unlike you but still walked, talked, thought, sought, sat, smelled, and sensed like you, but was different. Thus appeared woman. Out of the birth of the rib-of-knowingness came, at first, the supposition that you were "this." But the recognition that you were not "this," that you were something beyond your mentality, gave you the confidence to deny "this" and still have your experience marked with meaning!

This is the dexterity and virtuosity that is an accompanying feature of the artistic element in evidence of those who are truly statesmen of the Light. It has always been pointed to in the statement, "to be one of them and not *of* it,"or "to appear to be in their midst but not *of* it." *The puzzle seems to have so many parts, but when the Center knows it is the Center, it does not mind how long the others take to find it. The only thing about the Center is, it is satisfied; the parts never are. That is why if "you" are satisfied and sit, you achieve nothing.*

"Serene I fold my hands and wait" is satisfaction resulting in deterioration. What is deterioration? The *blurring* of the intention.

This "Work" (as it appears to be called for convenience), this *Unfoldment*™ which you experience as realignment, is really no longer for those who are unprepared. The only thing that marks my interest is to see the Plan being harmonically fulfilled in the rhythm and the joy of the song that has been termed *given to Praise.*

You who find others who are attuned to this mystery, this natural wonder included within your very Soul-Force, should be ever observant of those who cognize you. The time is so short for others to recognize your statesmanship. Your studentship is secondary, for your studentship is *seeing;* your statesmanship is *hearing.* It is the second level and the only one that is required before you enter into the higher echelon where you start to move intuitively with the precision of the Rockettes! No one can dance with God with the rhythm of His Being and still have his foot in his mouth. He must find the Heart on his tongue. *Too many of you make foul excuses instead of wise announcements.*

You should put an end to your tendencies that interfere with synchronized movement commensurate with the dance of the divine. You do not enter into a stream of activity from the standpoint of entering when you feel like it!

You cannot have fidelity to half a dozen things. Your inclination is to be flat-out, but that table is only for the pieces. When you start to put your puzzle together, what was flat on the surface bears the dimensions as if it existed in space. That is exactly what you are like! You were nothing but a seed particle flat-out, hidden from view, but your imagination and the wonder of nurturing your imagination brought you forth as the evidence of the continuity of Being!

> **Realignment is not the assertion**
> **of impeccable statements.**
> **It is the radiance of attainment.**

Do not allow your mind to make a statement dulled by the intellect. Do not try to say something impressive. *Be* expressive! There are enough Monets. They create an impression; yours is expression. An impression is that "you" are.

Do you feel radiance?

Students) Yes, Sir.

Does it *go?*

Students) No, Sir.

It certainly appears to go! Therefore, you know your *"mind"* is telling you what is radiance and what is not.

Your "highfalutin" statements are usually just a waste of breath. (You know, like a breathy flute player.) It is not your "highfalutin" statements that matter; it is your ability to withdraw the nail of doubt from the coffin of your mind!

Use the teeth of Truth to withdraw the nail of doubt from your mind, which manufactures your coffin, the container of a dead body.

> **What is a dead body? One that cannot respond. When you cannot respond, you are dying. When you cannot have the fire and the vitality in your declaration and presence, it shows there is a lack in the validity of your attainment.**

You have to know, no matter where you are, you *are* the State that you hold to be well-defined, beyond your intellect and its rampage-like tendencies.

Refrain from playing an intellectual game with anyone and watch how bored he becomes. Do not try to convince anyone else of your uniqueness. Let your activity evidence that. Do not try to enlighten anyone, because there is no-one to enlighten.

You can see how it is that a part can be played that seems important for you who are having to define your markings clearly. My Mark cannot be defined, it can only be known, because it never is the same. *It changes instantaneously. This has always been the very seed of discontent for those who wanted to blur their definition of purpose in my life.* "Mr. Mills is always changing his mind." **Would you not have thought that somebody would have perceived that if I can change my mind, you should not have *it*?** My mind has never been in an unchangeable condition. The mind? I do not even know what it is. I am told it is; I do not mind. I am told I am "this"; I do not care.

Some people say, "You have all your degrees." I say, "I have no degrees, but you can bestow them on me!" It does not make a particle of difference. Some of you spend years getting doctorates. *Who cares?* What is a doctorate to a carrot, if it does not know it contains carotene and vitamin A? **What is the point of a doctorate if you do not know the essential ingredient of your Being?**

What do you suppose is the purpose of language? Do you suppose it is to emit a tonality that others cognize as a universal pitch? Why is it important to be positioned before you speak? If you are not positioned *before you speak,* your *position* speaks; *it* is better *without* "you," because *it* certainly cannot be found *within* "you."

Without "you," I AM. If I AM without "you," *I* cannot be within "you." Because if I AM without "you," there is no "you" to be within. Therefore, *I* cannot be confined by association with a limited objective form.

If I AM without "you," *I* cannot be within "you"; therefore, *I include* you, for you have been part of a selected force to exemplify a pattern and a Plan for a universal solvent when the parts are fitly joined together as a result of a clear definition of purpose, and the table is prepared to receive the parts on the sacrificial altar of transcendency.

I have told you there was another Commandment. There were ten, but the eleventh one is "Make an altar of Earth." The Earth is the holy place and must be restored, for it was the source of all wonder to the truly aboriginal.

Why bother with definitions, if it is not to define the incredible purpose of appearance? That is the great promise, if you are of that culture that believes in a promise. Many in this culture do not believe in a promise, but if you do, then it says, "*I* will never leave you." Impossible! For *I* was never in "you" or without "you." *I* was never within you or *without* you! That is why there is such solace found in the consolation of a song termed "The

Sound of a Star."[2] It caused a rift in the mentality so that the mind could be adopted and adapted to the statesmanship becoming this Age.

Those who have left this association think, upon leaving, they have chosen a way to become equal to this, but instead of a continuing wellspring unto their life, there is a supposition that they are persons gaining an intellectual persuasion from various streams.

Water considered as H_2O never satisfies your thirst. As an icicle it can appear, as steam it can appear, and it can be condensed as dew. Unless it is freed from the abstract formulation of a theory, it does not bear the fructifying power that is commensurate with an authentic experience.

This has to do with what appears as thought bearing the attention that wipes your slate clean of limitations. You write upon your slate your limitations. *You cannot have these incongruities appearing in your life.* Can you imagine people being late, overeating, being moody? You can name it all. It has nothing to do with what I AM.

These characteristics do not mark statesmanship. You cannot involuntarily be the radiance if you are trying to impress someone. Perhaps if you *expressed,* that someone you are trying to impress would feel the pressure of Presence to adopt what is known as the promise. The universal solvent is not just Love but the force of Truth to extricate all impediments from the field of your intellectual endowments.

The future of the people of any nation depends upon the people of that nation adopting and adapting a new precision for **marking the meaning of their presence with the individuality commensurate to the universality of a piece of work that evidences the artistry of the divine.**

---

2. "The Sound of a Star," a poem by Kenneth G. Mills, *Anticipations* (Toronto: Sun-Scape Publications, 1980); read by the poet with musical accompaniment on *The Tonal Garment of The Word* (Sun-Scape Records, KGOC/D33). Also recorded by The Star-Scape Singers conducted by Kenneth G. Mills on *The Sound of a Star* (Sun-Scape Records, KGOM18).

This is what you have entertained all these years. If I never speak to you again, you should know that this is what has been going on in the simplicity of Kenneth Mills. How simple have *you* been?

In my simplicity, you found me. In your complexity, how many have found you?

The simplicity of Being is a spontaneous creativity, appearing garmented in wonder-sounds of an inexplicable nature. They are heard. To answer "How?" is without "you" and yet with "you." You have elected such a State to be present in order to extricate your *yearnings* from your *earnings* of materiality.

Your leanings should be not to the lean-to of a temporary housing but to the ordered foyer in preparation for a Light audience.

▼

Chapter IV

The Gracious Nature of Discovery

knowledge

oral tradition

discovery

Realignment

Truth

The Gracious Nature of Discovery

We are in the throes of a new beginning and in the throes of birthing facts, not fiction.

Do you need to know what you are?

Students) Yes, Sir.

If you know what you are, is it necessary to prolong what you are not?

Students) No, Sir.

**What you *are* is a discovery;
what you *are not* is obvious!**

It is stated in the ancient books that Truth is never *discovered*. Truth is a *discovery*. What Truth IS is unlimited, for it is infinite; it is always a discovery. The reason you talk so much about what *isn't* is because you have discovered, and anything that is discovered is unreal. What you have discovered is always up for questioning. What is discovered is always changing and demanding explanation. Truth is always a discovery,[1] never bearing any need of explanation, for it is not something you can lay your hands on.

> **Truth is discovery.**
> **Truth is revealment.**
> **Revealment is the evidence of Truth.**
> **What is discovered and objectified is part of**
> **your dream network.**

When you have discovered that you have made a mistake, you know it because of the discovery that another made to *reveal* the mistake. Truth is always revealing so that there is no concealment of error.

The purpose of perceiving subtlety is so that you will be apart from attempting to gain knowledge about what is discovered. That would be ignorance. Why would you attempt to gain knowledge about what is discovered?

> Paul S.) To attempt to fortify a false existence?

To attempt to fortify a false existence. That is why knowledge accumulates about the discovered. *There is no knowledge about Truth.*

The discovered goes into chaos; Truth reveals you are attempting to be knowledgeable. The attempt to be knowledgeable about the discovered is chaos. It is *chaos* when you think the knowledge of what is discovered will reveal Truth. It will not!

Why do you meditate constantly? Why is meditation a constant? It is always a discovery. To enter into oblivion in meditation is a false panacea for doing it. I was saying to a

---

1. The Latin root of "discovery" means "to reveal."

man this evening that *God rests in action!* He said, "My word! I've never heard that statement before." *God rests in action!* That is a discovery which none of *you* have had yet! Why is everyone so vehement in sustaining a knowledgeable position about a discovery, about a revelation? What does a revelation signify?

David N.) It signifies something new.

Exactly! But not something new about something old. That is why there is such misapprehension about revelation. A revelation is about something new, not old. Therefore, in the Book of Revelation it is revealed that characterization and symbolization point to the knowledge gained; those symbols and characters are nothing but an attempt to bring to light what they reveal, from the standpoint of knowledge. What they reveal is that they do not exist in discovery. They are only there to hold the mind in the vise, in the throes of birthing beyond them.

Birthing is newness appearing. It never stops. Birthing never ceases. Birthing is a garment discovery wears. That is why it is said, "When I come again, I will make all things new!" That is a symbolic utterance of knowledge. It is not a symbolic statement of meaning unless you can translate it through discovery. This is why **Man exists as the evidence of discovery; men and women exist as the discovered!** If men and women exist as the discovered, they attempt to gain knowledge to substantiate the things that go with the discovered.

If Truth is a discovery, it cannot bear any relation whatsoever to a fluctuating condition. That is why it is said, "I AM the same yesterday, to-day, and forever," because I AM a discovery.

Since Truth is a discovery, can it be aged?

Students) No, Sir.

This is why Truth, as a discovery, is so important. If one Synonym is a discovery, all Synonyms of God are a discovery! Therefore, God is not gained by knowledge, for knowledge is about the thing and God is not a thing. Therefore, the knowledge of God is thought-knowledge, or thought-facts put into the thought-thing, or the thought-object, or the thought-divine: God!

If all the seven Synonyms of God are now known to be a discovery, then the entire experience of Man as the image and likeness of God is discovery! To the discovered, that is termed "spontaneous expression." To discovery, nothing has happened. *God rests in action!*

You tentatively hold this plane within the confines of your gathered information, scholastically codified according to the objectification and the classification of the things. As long as you hold to "this," you are holding to a suppositional existence. A suppositional existence needs support, as do the legs of the living dead. The living dead are those who bear no response.

What is the difference between a live body and a dead body?

Students) Response!

You can only testify to your discovered bodies. Discovery is timeless; the discovered is timed. Love is timeless; discovered, it seems to fluctuate. Mind, a discovery, is forever new; Mind objectified goes with a body sustained by food and a mind sustained by thoughts. Without thought there is no mind, but that does not mean to say there is no Consciousness. That which *says* "no mind" is obviously the Consciousness that IS. If there is no mind, I live, even when I appear to have one. *You* wonder if I do! **God rests in action!**

Every time you personalize your activity, you are attempting to overthrow and move into an arena of dialectics where, through your knowledge of historical data, you attempt to be impressive in the presentation of the discovered Truth of the Bible, of all the sacred writings.

The reason the Truth of all sacred writings is the same is because it is a discovery, not open to the destruction of knowledge. If the seven Synonyms likened unto God are claimed through the practice of associating only with those thoughts that are in keeping with the "knowledgeable" conditions ascribed unto a Godhood, then the practice is to subject the objecting thought-forms to the power of thoughts that annul the opposition. That is only for practice; not one bit of good is done by it.

> **If you do not have control over your thoughts in practice, you have no spontaneous artistic persuasion evidencing discovery!**

If Truth were discovered, there would be no quest! If God were discovered, there would be no need . . to understand God. How can a mind, which lives on thoughts, discover God which is the source or essence of Life, Truth, Love, Mind, Spirit, Soul? Is it not justifiably exclaimed "incredible!"? It is the most *creditable* State, and *incredible* to the discovered!

Why do people attempt to refer to the past in order to bring a vibrancy to the present, if it is not in the pattern of knowledge: "I want you to know I experienced that but you did not"? "I know more than you know." "You haven't lived as long I have. Therefore, you could not possibly know what it is like, so don't bother saying too much yet, you're too young." *Discovery has nothing to do with age! Discovery has to do with being authentic and allowing the discovered to evidence a visible "stand-in" until the Invisible is known to be an authentic situation by discovery.*

Truth is never discovered in the East,
        the North, the South, or the West,
For Truth is where *I* is addressed!

Assert the *I* and find Truth a discovery with no need of
I. *The only value of I is to give you a buoy, constructed of
thoughts, that you hold in the motherlode commensurate
with Deity.*

There is no "if" condition, no "but" condition in discovery, but in the discovered there are many butts to kick!
I do not know why you do not leave the "buts" behind!
This type of word supplies such a contrived pattern of alteration. You contrive patterns of alteration through the use of
words such as "if," "but," "why," "when," "wherefore,"
"whereto," "maybe." All of these words provide fodder for
the discovered in the hopes of gaining knowledge of the
ancient Scriptures.

The ancient Scriptures are the evidence that knowledge
has not discovered Truth but that Truth exists. The knowledge that there is Truth is codified, but Truth itself is not
exemplified because it is not in a dimension of perspective
and mass. Therefore, Truth is not timed!

That is why Life, Truth, Love, Spirit, Mind, Soul, God
are eternal; in other words, they have nothing to do with
time but are only known through discovery. Every book of
holy Scripture that contains a Truth is the evidence of the
undying and gracious nature of discovery. It allows what
isn't to appear to hold the attention until what IS is *experienced* as discovery!

What a Corporation to have back of you! You do not
need to think you stand alone. You have the entire corporate
structure "discovered" dropped into the tonality of discovery, which means spontaneous expression that puts an end
to the attempt to create impressions.

Impressions go with the visionary. The Vision is never
veiled. We say Truth is veiled. Why? To discover after all

these years of bodification that you are Conscious-Being, God-endowed here and now, is a tremendous blow to knowledge! You thought you were going to gain your freedom by knowledge, and all you have gained is an intellectual bondage.

Discovery could reduce the mortality rate because Truth, Life, Love (the Synonyms) as a discovery are a continuing rhythmic wave of wonder. You cannot discover it; it can only be experienced as discovery. The Synonyms of God can never be discovered, only as characters like those used in printing; they can only be known in discovery.

The discovered is always *terminal*. Discovery has no beginning or end! This is why, they say, Truth lives eternally, Love lives eternally, God lives eternally, Soul lives eternally, Mind lives eternally, Spirit lives eternally, Principle lives eternally.

Maybe you will see. To reiterate Truth is to stabilize the characterized forms of Truth within the unstable thought-fields. When Truth is a discovery, the stabilizing has only been a suffering to be so until *I* come and then "*I* make all things new," which means what?

> **Truth as a discovery is always new,**
> **and that is associated with *I*.**
> **I only exist as a character discovered.**
> **The Life-force is discovery!**

What you have just heard is the evidence of discovery. When you rehear it, you will be *hearing!* This is why it is on such a level of attainment. Regardless of what anyone says, this is why the oral tradition is so important, because *the oral tradition is a Sound discovery*. It cannot be theory adapted to your species; it has to be allowed to appear to be contained in knowledge until you have the confidence to be living without "maybe." That takes away any possibility of missing spring! *This is a new beginning!*

What has been said should be listened unto, but do not attempt to talk about it because you will make it *discovered*. Let it be *living* as discovery. How do you find an oral or sound Transmission living as a Teacher? By discovering what it is like to live as he does! That will transcend the discovered. As the Tibetan nun said, "It is impossible to consider that you are giving this uncontradictable Teaching in English. In the most dualistic language, you are giving an absolute Transmission. In Tibet, it has not been given in over three thousand years. I cannot believe I am hearing it in the West!"

If it is uncontradictable, what is it? *It has to be experienced!* How? As a discovery! This is all the clue I will give. What is a clue? It is a key to discovery.

When discovery is your experience, it is noted by another as something discovered.

If you are discovered, what you are in essence is the discovery!

When you go on a trip to the far East or to the far North or to the far South or to the far West, why do you go?

Gregory S.) To see something new.

You said it right: to **see** something new. You seldom do! Landscape is landscape; bodies are bodies; water is water; birds are birds; food is food; thoughts are thoughts; cars are cars; horses are horses; pigs are pigs; sheep are sheep; goats are goats; wagons are wagons; hay is hay; nightmares are nightmares! Why do you continue to feed them the hay? You were supposed to have gotten rid of that mattress! It was one thing to have a nightmare when you had a hay mattress. That is why they were called "nightmares": you fed them from your mattress of sleep! (Hay was in the mattress!) If in your dream state you knew enough to feed your nightmare, what are you feeding your daydream if it is not the substance of your attention? This is why your attention has to be filled with what is termed "the *Christ*ened Nathanael."

Nathanael was one who was known by Jesus for his talent, the "imagination." It is said in the holy books that there must be a *Christ*ened Adam in the New Age, in the fulfillment of the new promise. It is not quite accurate; to me it seems it should be the *Christ*ened *Nathanael*. Nathanael points to the imagination, and when the imagination is *Christ*ened, it holds control over what you imagine and precipitate! An unredeemed imagination produces an unredeemed experience. It is a *redeemed* imagination that frees you from "imagining vain things."

This is why anyone who is doing film work or anyone who is a choreographer or anyone who is an architect, anyone who is bearing a mark of artistry, must move from the standpoint of expression that has been held under the rein of an ordered, rhythmic Light-happening, so that when the objective is precipitated, it does not need to be edited!

I am so glad I looked at Nisargadatta's book, because all that he gave to one man was the sentence: "Truth is a discovery."

If you are exhausted from your work, it is obvious you are not doing anything! That is why it is so tiring. "You" cannot do anything, but as long as you think "you" can do something, it is exhausting. *God rests in action!* Personalize it, and what do you have? "Oh, dear, what can the *matter* be?" It may be waiting for May Day, the day that the newness of the divine births. *It is not an invasion; it is an appropriation of the nowness of Being authentic.*

Why do you always keep the facets of a jewel clean? So that any one facet may reflect the Light to someone who is waiting to see expression! To *hear* expression! Now maybe you understand why the Bible says, "Having ears ye hear not and eyes ye see not what I have to tell unto the people" — unto the *prepared*!

This is Realignment! It has nothing to do with religion; in essence, it has nothing to do but realign you to what you really are. That is the living discovery of the seven Synonyms sounding, on the seven strings, the diapason of Being and the dominant fact that *I* can be found, if you are willing to move from the leading tone to the higher and not drop back to the past for comfort.

There is no comfort zone in the past. It could be filled with fear and trepidation. There is no comfort zone in the future. There is only the nowness of discovery. You appear to live and to move and to be healthy, wealthy, and wise, all in the semblance of "you" and "me" as we disguise the new discovery that *revealing is the possibility of realignment to the eternal!*

That's That!

> **What is the purpose of a statesman?**
> **It is to state, in the name of Man,**
> **the government that is in residence with**
> **the discovery of Truth!**

You all have this as part of your agenda. Your words must not be seasoned with "April in the rain" or "dancing in the tulips," unless you *know* how to cause each one that is still a bud to blossom.

You must be able to elucidate with simplicity and sincerity the experience of *your* discovery, not mine! If you cannot speak naturally about it, you will never speak factually about what appears even as "Mr. Mills." You will make what is natural a sharp or a flat, because you will go with the tonality in which you find yourself instead of establishing the Pitch commensurate with discovery. This is very important, for you are *marked.*

No one can tell you what your markings are. Anyone who tells you what your marking is, is *not* telling you what your marking is! It is a supposition that he even knows what your marking is! Your marking has to be a discovery, and it is never done intellectually. Discovery bypasses the intellect, yet allows it to be utilized to point the way to the center, *the center and the circumference of Being.* The blazing wheels of Ezekiel are no longer in the heavens but are within those thought-arenas so that the spectacle of revealment appears as a risen Fire, embracing the circumference of your ability to radiate from the hub or the center of your wheel.

A miracle is nothing but the lessening of the objective confinement and, to others, it is wonder! The exegesis of all that has happened is not open to the knowledge realm but is known by the knowledge realm to be a threat. For when man knows what IS, he leaps off the ledge of knowledge and allows "the remains" to be a tonal encounter. *This is the statesman of the future.*

> The statesman of to-morrow is a tonal encounter, bearing the pitch of Reality bearing universal significance.
>
> As Being, my life appears, and others say "centered." The performance is the form that it takes to allow another to see the artistic element of fundamental wonder coming forth as performance.
>
> The artistry of Being is the spontaneous expression of an unmediated current of wonder precipitated into your realm of expectation in order to marvel!

▼

Chapter V

The Diapason of Transcendent Worth

thought/mind

fulfillment

art/artist

energy

divine activity

I AM

The Diapason of Transcendent Worth

What am I?
Who am I?
Where am I?

"What am I?" "Who am I?" "Where am I?" Do any of you people ever have these questions?

Students) Yes, Sir.

It is worthless! Worthless. You are trying to find the whereabouts and the maybes surrounding ignorance. When you declare you are Miss Toebuckle or Mrs. Kneebuckle or Mrs. Beltbuckle or Miss Unshoelace, it is absolutely ridiculous. You are trying to establish ignorance or the dream into a pattern that is *possible!* Ignorance spends hours sitting in the presence of Teachers, expecting to find enlightenment. You will no sooner answer one question about ignorance than another arises, because ignorance is based on questions and answers that are inaccurate. Unless it is Truth, the source from which each arises bears no power to rescind the suggestion.

Have you noticed how most of your questions arise from "you" as if you *were* "this"? Have you noticed how most of your activity is done as if it were "yours"? Have you noticed that most of what you do is exhausting because "you" do it? What are people doing to-day? Searching for jobs. Why do they seldom find one that is exactly what they want? Because what they *want* is in *need*. If it is in need, it is not true!

By these rather ridiculous questions and statements, you can perceive that Truth is discovered, for it reveals the fallacious! *Every moment Truth is being your experience, what isn't is confronted, because what isn't does not have power, other than what you give it by the arsenal of thoughts that you explode in an eruption of ego and resentment and jealousy. What a myth! This is why it might be said that Truth is a discovery that reveals the fanciful nature. This does not mean that the fanciful nature does not exist; Truth just points out that it is not Real.* You can never find water where there is none. Why would you expect to find Truth, Love, wisdom, insight where there is none? It *cannot* be in the desert of the mind!

The only reason you have a moment of fulfillment is because in that moment "you" cease to be so present. As soon as "you" became present, you were your same unsatisfied, questioning, personalized, personified exasperation, hunting for work. *You* cannot ever expect to find work.

Being is not work. God rests in action!

The whole root of the penury of the world is "you are" instead of "I AM," and that is what should be penned upon your Scroll of remembrance. **The pen-"you"-ry is because "you" are eerie!** "You" are! "You" are a figment of the imagination, made to feel substantial by adoration, by having someone love you. Unless somebody loves you as the Love that IS, it is never satisfying, it is spasmodic. God is not spasmodic, neither is Truth spasmodic; Being is not spasmodic; the seven Synonyms of God are not spasmodic, either they would not have borne a tale through all the beliefs of years.

How can you find an answer to the world's problems?

Gregory S.) You cannot from the world standpoint.

Not at all! You cannot, and yet the leaders of the world *think* they are the leaders of the world. Spell the word "lead" for me.

Students) L-e-a-d.

Heavy, is it not? There is no solution to the world's problems from the leadership of those imbued with a false identity. Why is everything so slow? Because of leaders with lead in their pants and thought where it should not be! In their heads? The mind lives on thought, and yet "brainology" now tells us there is absolutely no proof found that thoughts are in the brain. They are not; they have nothing to do with the brain! The brain evidences the energy that a thought is, which is a particle of a continuing stream of omniaction, but *thought* interrupted! Thought interrupted creates a form. **As long as thought is not interrupted, it is not thought, it is energy.** The essence, the fabric of the Synonyms, interrupted creates "a sin," and that is why it can be said, "Man is born in sin."

The contrived Earth experience is an interrupted prelude until relieved in the Light of the divine activity. *A prelude signifies the beginning, but to find that Truth is a discovery, there is no beginning and there is no end. There is only a beginning and an end to what is discovered and what discovers!*

If there is a huge forum to consider what is to be done with the fulminating spots in the world, the fermenting mentalities evidencing themselves, and the fervent prayer of some to see peace restored, what is to be done but to allow them all to be reduced to what they are! *Then the table is cleared for the puzzle of the world to be reassembled. Being reassembled can appear only as a result of Being assembled!*

> **Meaning reduces the problem to a dream.**
> **When the dream *is not,* Day IS!**

Where are you found in the avenues of time? What is the value of Being found? It reduces the avenue to the straight and narrow, and few enter thereat. Why is the straight and narrow Path so described? It is the simplest way to say, **"Intention must be clearly defined."** Intention defined to the mind gets out of the pages of your mental dictionary by the evidence of your directed movement, bearing the cognition of your emancipated state. When one is emancipated, one is set free. To what have you been bound in the slave market of to-day? The lord of your mind, which is the black market!

It is an incredible consideration: **How many are in league with the black forces that use the mind that is *not* emancipated to *appear* to be emancipated, only to *mine* the Path that is termed "straight and narrow"?** If revealment is perceived, supposition has to fade, and the suppositional support system of your incarceration disintegrates by the restoration of the continuing stream of uninterrupted inspiration. The stream is so great, it allows its tributaries to appear as an enlightened offering wherever you may be found.

> **An inspired message is *breathed;***
> **it is *not thought!***

A thought-out message is mind-full, and the resulting need of dogma and the pervasiveness of fear enhance the lack of clarity and try to give it credence by formulation and forums.

You appear, so someone has told you, and what accompanies "you" is an appendage to sustain, in an appendage of suggestions, a dying supposition prolonged by a belief system. *How is a belief system born? By associating facts with fiction. It is continued by a belief in a continuing choice.*

If it is truly the Day, it is the one "that the Lord hath made. Rejoice and be glad therein," for it is the irradiance of an uninterrupted Light which carries in its might a way from belief.

> *Who is ready for such rarefied sound waves?*
> Those that bear a clearly defined intention, which annihilates the static of the mind!
>
> *What causes the static?*
> Associating the thought-patterns with logic in order to fortify an unstable, theoretical position, thus bringing about the deterioration in the ranks of those bearing the possibility of sounding a diapason of transcendent worth!
>
> *What is the value of perceiving a symbol if it is not to move beyond it and see its diamond-worth nature?!*

People have said, "What is that symbol in the diamond pendant you wear?" I said, "It is my name, it is my initials." They said, "What?! Those are your initials?" I said, "Yes, before the alphabet that you now know." It was just a symbol, but now it is clad and cast and set in diamonds, bearing, in spite of the surety of the present alphabet, the purity of the uncontaminated origin pointing to an attempt to communicate.

If there are the remains, there remains a mystery, and that mystery is: "Where did it come from?" How can you answer from the standpoint of being part of the dream sequence? It is impossible, but the dynamics are present that reduce the suggestion and allow the exhibit of artistry to be perceived.

Freed from your limits, the artistry of Being allows you to appear an artist in order to break the mesmerism surrounding art. What is the purpose of the art of Being? It is artless and the very ground from which all of the seeds of Light appear to spring in order to hold your attention until *"I spring"* appears on your calendar of events. Then I AM found not a seasonal happening but an eternal round. For discovery, the circumference is never known, the radius is never known, and the point is never felt. Others delineate it symbolically in order for you to have courage to ride the razor's edge, have a foot in each world, and yet be a colossus beyond the scholarship of Rhodes. A giant strides o'er the intervals.[1] How can you detect an interval if the Source is not pitch?

How can you detect what is not, if the Source is not All and cognized as such? You may say, "Nothing!" but look at the Something that the nothing points to. What allowed ignorance of language to point to the allness of Being? Nothing! The Nothingness allows the somethingness to satisfy the cry for food from those who do not realize that it is a suggestion on the straight and narrow, when the gates are opened. Discussion allows "cussin'." When you cuss about what is not, you fill the way with the "potholes" of your system. No one else, thank goodness, steps into them unless you have generated a following.

The amazing experience called "this" allows what *isn't* to appear to enjoy it. For the appearance to appear to enjoy it shows that the apparent joy is only in appearance. That is why joy is only an echo. It is a figment of the imagination, as is happiness, as is pain, as is sorrow, as is want, as is anything

---

1. See the poem "Giant" by Kenneth G. Mills, *Anticipations* (Toronto: Sun-Scape Publications, 1980), p. 100.

until "*I come*" makes the appearance of all things new. You have witnessed how it may be done beyond the April showers, which do bring May flowers, and you find it clad in the joy of spring. What is the value of a spring? It allows one to be thrown. Where will you land? In the web of the mind or in the lap of the Infinite?

Thank you.

Now you can see why questions are worthwhile. They allow you to wait until *I come*. Such simplicity in the most complex structure of what are termed, for language's sake, "planes" or "vibratory frequencies"! Remember, a plane or an octave of Being has nothing whatsoever to do with distance; it has to do with vibrational frequencies. That is the only way you can describe it for you. But what if the "you" were not like "you"? What if you is really not like "you," which it is not? Then you can appear to be "you" in the likes of "you" while you remain as I AM. Why do we say "as I AM"? It is complete.

I AM does not require an object; it signifies a permanent State with an identity, a perfect capsulation of a static state. In this rendition of this rhapsody of Being, the static state is broken when it is revealed that God rests in action. The statement "I AM" is only stopped as a sentence until you realize that in the revealment the AM is always active and known as the AM-ing of the I. Right in the symbol "AM" is the "-i-n-g" of the creativity of Being. So, the I AM looks static, but if you tune to the right frequency, it is the activity of omnipresent action, resting in its own allness. Until you perceive it, you think it is a statement of divinity; it is nothing but a lure to unlimited creativity!

How many colors are there in the rainbow?

Student) Seven.

How do you cause them to sound? By playing upon the discovery of the seven Synonyms of God being an art form and yet formless. Remember, Beethoven lived for many years with an irascible uncle who imbibed too much and frequently returned from the court inebriated. He would be so miserable to Beethoven that Beethoven realized the way to get even was to allow his uncle to go to bed, and then, upon hearing him snore, go downstairs and play not a triad (that would not have awakened him); he played a dominant seventh! And the uncle, being such a musician even in his drunken stupor, would have to go down and resolve it!

Remember, you have the seven Synonyms because of a prism, but when they are perceived and definable, it is known that the prism has been the *diamond*. That is how in India they call it "the achievement of the glowing diamond." They call it "the crest jewel of discrimination." It allows discrimination, but it is the light of the Unlimited passing through the crystal clarity that causes all crystal to melt. What must you discriminate? Only one demand:

Are you "this"
or Am I That?

When you know I AM That, how can you ask, "Am I That?" You are sentenced! Now you can see, the only place you are bound is within the mind. The only place you are free is in Being That!

▼

To find the Event of significance in the midst of your non-significance, you must see that the change that is demanded is a radical one. To have a radical change is to see everything from a new perspective!

"In the Sunlight of Grace"

"What flows from
the Center is the drop
of pristine clarity, and
what reaches the outer rim
is the pristine clarity diluted
by the tincture of belief."
– Kenneth George Mills

wrong language emotionalized!
Sonics of destruction by
all part of a spectrum of the Unsee...
— give them so many colors
Words — give them a vibrating, sonic Intent
... into a vibrating, sonic Intent
Race of Man ... waiting to be
has declared ...
The oracle
can only be the sun
The Source
messenger o...
Wing
of Su...
Ben...

Divine Facts
I AM not thought
and That is That —
The razor's edge —
fragrance ...
Take the courage ...
the nature of the flower
How fragrant are the...
of your garden?
You are not "this" —
You are not to be That?
but how do you play the part
If you cannot play it in hell
you will have to direct it in hell

BIRTH OF BEING
Act of Being divine
Nobility of your
second birth
Perfection allows you
to see imperfection
Dare to live as the divine
on this stage called the Earth
How can you know from the stage
of time what your part is?
'Tis only to BE the invisible
Rider to time
Harness the errant mind — Your mind ... is cluttered
with facts that bear only fiction as root

...ight
...race
...er of the
...c of the Light
...adiance —
...ancy of Principle
The Sun shines
on one and all
Alphabet — an
palescent spectrum of Light
here are you in the panoply of Light?
...ines as "you" depends upon the state of your mind
Shadows trying to say they live

mandala: a symbolic circular
figure representing the universe

Chapter VI

In the Sunlight of Grace

procrastination

drama

glamour

second birth

well of abundance

radiance

Love

In the Sunlight of Grace

We are gathered together in the Sunlight of grace,
And in the cognition of divine facts we dare to take
      on an enactment of grace.
We dare to rescind the suggestions of mind
And attempt to transcend the alphabet of time
By delineating in words all those that appeal
To that part of the nature that is transitory and
      does not appeal
To the stability of Being found without doubt,
Lodged and supported in the heart of Love.

We peruse the fields of time and declare,
"This is our stage for enactment if we dare!"
We take the perception of a "you" and a "me"
And find the direction is to trust in your deed.

How can you know from the stage of time
What your part is if your thought is not authentic,
      attributable to the divine?
You can say, "I'm this poor hunk of meat in
      this clay —
And yet I appear to walk this Earth-stage way.

"I sometimes sleep and I sometimes don't
And I sometimes complain and I'm sometimes
      broke!
I'm sometimes up and I'm sometimes down,
And my nose itches in the Earthian round!"

But when you can stay in position and see,
'Tis the wonder of the magic of the Light indeed.
It allows the finger to itch the nose,
It allows the tongue to parade, as it shows
The words that are not etched on any calendar of
      time,
But are utilizing the alphabet in the Light divine!

Every word that you take points to the gleaming
      fact
That you are not "this" — but how do you dare to
      be That?!
You have to take the courage to drop this mortal
      thought
That you are this human being, slung in a bag
      which you are and yet you are not!

How can you find imperfection in perfection in
      deed?
You can't, you idiot! It is perfection that allows you
      to see the imperfect act; it is no *deed!*
It is the natural State, it is the State divine.
Why don't you harness the errant mind?!

What are you doing in this vale of doubt?
The Sunshine is giving this grace about,
And we can see there is no shadow but a dance.
Is it the Light that is trembling, or the shadows that
      seem to prance
On the wall of appearance on your stage of doubt?
Is it the Light that is trembling, or just the shadows

trying to say they *live* because of the steady
Light that is about?

The lake in its serenity, the air so free,
The leaves, they dance on the tree in tremulous
        glee.
The lake, it laughs when it sees a leaf so quake.
You would think it was going to be baptized in the
        Light for the water's sake!

But the leaf is graced to receive without doubt
The benediction of the Sunshine about.
The magic takes place in its leaf, as you know,
And the chlorophyll is formed, and so green it
        glows.

Why don't you take the courage and gain the hue
That becomes the nature of the Real? Will you?
Why don't you assert that your "I" can be found,
But you have to pretend on this Earthly round?

Then in the act of Being divine,
You attempt to enact it on the stage of the mind.
And then see what happens, and what will be
        shall be.
There is no question! That is why Shakespeare is
        without his deed.
He gave you a promise: "To be or not to be." But
        there was doubt;
He gave you a choice. There is no more choice
        about.

Why do you dance within the mind
Of thinking: "I'm secure and I wasn't, one time.
I agreed to come and I agree to go
But I still love what *isn't* and yet I love What IS.
        Oh, such woe!"?

"*Whoa!*" to the mind that would "gee" to the left,
And "whoa!" to the mind that would "gee" to the
    right.
And where, what, is left?

"*A droit! A droit!*" is all one says in frenetic shouts
To the driver who is doubtful of the way
That I must find, in the act of Being divine.
Where is your freedom? In your mind?!

Your mind is cluttered with culture of time;
It is cluttered with knowledge that isn't divine.
It is cluttered with facts that bear only fiction as
    root,
And yet you go around all dressed up in your shoes
    and your boots!

As if you are geared. Which one do you use?
The low, or first gear? Why would you choose?
Take the fifth gear and move and say, "Those who
    doubt an interval in time,
What is sounding is the tonic, and the fifth gets you
    going, it is divine!"

Why are you so filled with woe and despair?
Have you built your life upon these humans?
    They're not rare.
There is not only one to Love in this time.
If there is, my God, you're caught in the mortal
    mind!

What is the mark of a free one in time?
    Love embraces all!
It is the act of Love, 'tis divine!
The one imprisoned in "immortal" clay —
O what a foolish word to use in an alphabet of
    the day!

There can never be an immortal to a mortal of
    time.
The word was used, and it didn't even trigger your
    mind.

You are so used to being cluttered in culture and
    knowledge galore,
But there is no glamour. There should be, for the
    eternal shore
Is filled with jewels, pristine and grand;
The inclusions in Earth had to be for a *hue*-man.
But when you find the world given back to the
    Source from which it sprung,
It is pristine, it is purity, it can only be sung!

Every time your love is just limited to one,
How can you be sure you're not just "a son of a
    gun"?
All love thought to be captured in time,
Is like trying to put salt on a wild bird of the mind!

Any love that you feel for one
Is only to satisfy the moment until you are flung
Into the lap of the Infinite and find,
God is Love and Love is God! Where is there a
    humankind?

Only parading for you to declare:
"Have the courage to take on the persona and dare
To live as the divine on this stage called the Earth."
Will you be termed "a Prince of the Sun" in your
    second birth?

Live now in the second, die now in the first,
And find there is no degree of Being.
There is only the razor's edge for others to see
How you walk on it and fall neither to one or the
    other, and yet you can be

On one or the other. You can dance, 'tis grand,
Because the horse of the mind is one, and it is
    saddled, for you dared.

The blanket of doubt is beneath your saddle of
    ease,
And the bridle of tenderness guides the mouth, as
    you please,
For every Word from this mouth should be seen as
    a fact
That it is conditioned to remove all the
    impediments of thought that is not fact.

Parade in the majesty and the glory of might.
Appear on this urge without any stage fright.
STOP allowing your mind to have the supremacy
    in your act in time.
STOP! and behold the grandeur at hand when your
    mind ceases to think and you experience "I
    AM."

I AM not thought! And that is That!
I AM not even "That," but 'tis a fact
That until I AM known and appear to enact,
"I AM That" is an *entr'acte.*

Then, after this moment of refreshment as planned,
You will see how you can appear to be an Earthian
    man.
In that moment of grandeur so kissed by the Sun —
It is the kiss of grace in the room that is One/won —
All geared to move in the rhythm divine,
And the mind like the horse trained in dressage, 'tis
    simply a wonder in time!

This is your act, and the oracle has declared:
"There are no fumes to seduce the mind that is clad

In the body of clay, seemingly on an Earthly round.
We have let the fumes fall from the thought of a
    language of time and are thereby not bound."
You can fume and you can fuss all you wish as you
    must;
Others will smell it, and you'll have to air it, I trust.

What is your state as you rejoice in the fact
That the Sun shines on one and all, *and it is not*
    tired in act?!
No leaf is unblessed, no apparent clod of the
    ground
Is unable to see and feel how the Sun shines,
    and grace is found.

Where are you in this panoply of Light?

Let me read you something that Puccini said:

> The inspiration from above stimulates the intellect and
> the emotions. An inspired person sees things in a totally
> different light than from one who is not inspired.
> Inspiration is an awakening, a quickening of all of man's
> faculties, and it is manifested in all high artistic achieve-
> ments. It is an overwhelming, compelling force. In short,
> it is a divine influence.[1]

Let me read you something else that Wagner said:

> I believe, first of all, that it is this universal vibrating
> energy that binds the soul of man to the Almighty
> Central Power from which emanates the life principle to
> which we all owe our existence. This energy links us to
> the Supreme Force of the universe, of which we are all a
> part. If it were not so, we could not bring ourselves into

---

1. Arthur M. Abell, *Talks with Great Composers* (New York: Carol Publishing
    Group, 1994), page 117.

communication with it. The one who can do this is inspired.[2]

Wagner said that he realized his revelations were of transcendental importance. He said:

> I feel that I am one with this vibrating Force, that it is omniscient, and that I can draw upon it to an extent that is limited only by my own capacity to do so.[3]

If you procrastinate, it is like anyone expecting a check to pay the rent or to pay your tithe and it does not come; days pass, and that check is already earmarked for something else. *Procrastination has brought about a depletion.* Always remember this!

Can you imagine a Savior-Principle going along with *your* mind and your condition? An ailing human? An oily human? A slippery human? A frenetic human? An obstreperous human? An ebullient human? It cannot go along with any of this, but without it "this" could not evidence those qualities. If it were not for perfection, you would not know that imperfection existed. That is how perfection (as we were reading the other day) "includes" imperfection — It does not *include* it; it *reveals* it! That is why the word in the book is wrong. Perfection does not *include* imperfection; it *reveals* imperfection.

With Pier Paolo I am always so impatient [referring to an architect friend]. I will say, "Pier Paolo, I would like all those drawings for the house by to-morrow morning!" It takes him weeks, the poor man! He has to have them put on the computer. He works it out; he cannot do it in a minute, but I always say it. Why? If I did not know the instantaneity of conception unconfined, I would say, "It's okay, Pier Paolo. Do it when you have time." As soon as I say that, I am limited!

---

2. *Ibid.*, p. 137.
3. *Ibid.*, p. 138.

That is the way anyone in business should operate: seemingly make the demand that goes with *nowness*. Even though it cannot be fulfilled, *expect* it to be fulfilled *before time!* It is the one way to keep the passage open. What is that passage? From sense to unlimited Substance. When you have unlimited Substance you have "US"!

Procrastination is the onset of the deterioration of wealth . . and health. Do you realize, "health" and "wealth" all come from the same root: "weal"? Penury is a state of a prophylactic nature. When there is penury, it is the onset or the first warning of a false allegiance, of a double allegiance. You cannot have two approaches to Substance or abundance. "The Well of Abundance" is not contaminated by hypotheses! "Penurious" means stingy, mean, lacking in generosity.

Where do you think the seeds have fallen? On the rich fertile soil of preparation, or on the sands? Where have the seeds of this revelation fallen? Have they fallen onto the rich soil of those prepared through tilling the soil of their intellectual achievement, turned over and turned over to receive the humus that will fecundate the seed kingdom that has been offered?

We know that the Cedars of Lebanon were so gigantic and so ageless. We also know that they were used in the building of the temple. We know also that they were the bearers of aroma or scent! Why scent? *Scent is the essence of freedom from limit!* It is the yielding of the gross to the Fire for translation, and thus, scent. It is termed "the fragrance of Being defined." *The fragrance of Being could appear as scent!* It is one of the key features of the new Epistle, for it points to the act of the rose in self-immolation. Upon giving itself up, with all its glamour, it reveals its transcendent worth as scent. For you who have doubted, even its ashes bear the fragrance for your drawers of the mind, for the cupboards of your thought, and for the sachets that would have your under-garments fragrant.

How fragrant are the flowers of your garden so that the potpourri offered is one of attraction, together with your radiance, together with the vibrancy of Principle, and the offering of inspiration to those expiring in the contaminated atmosphere of partial combustion? Why have oily rags? The ointment should have been to caress the feet. The oil should have been used to caress the body and the head, for it was the mark of consecration from the world of seduction to another cause.

"For this Cause came I," and if I say that, it is for you, not for me! So many re-cast the words unto me, when these words are cast to you. They are a gift of a life to you with your paltry offering of cognition, with your emaciated attempt to enact the nobility of your second birth, and the effrontery that has dared to parade in the face of an indisputable Light of your own divine nature! *You could not be here hearing this vocalization if it were not for your purpose and for your cause. The effect is neither here nor there, but BE and then the Cause is* **marked!**

> *BE*-Cause Love has made thee Mine, I'll cherish thee!
> Through floods of dismay and doubt found in time,
>   I'll carry thee.
> Though billows roar and bells proclaim,
> It is the tone of Love that prevails.
> Because God has made thee more than mind,
> I'll cherish thee.

That is how it appears that a puzzle can be placed upon your table, and the Center known, for Love has made thee more than mind, and for that reason it appears that *I cherish thee.* If you can perceive the puzzling effect of multiplicity, then you have to put it in its place on the altar of grace in the sunshine of your Soul.

> The annals of time have given unto men with minds
> Rituals and dogmas and creeds, in order to help
>   rein in the wild horse of the mind,

For it must be tamed with affection of its might
When it is harnessed for a purpose, which was to
      be a winged horse of Light.

It takes a Mercurian splendor to ride the winged
      horse and not be found a myth.

All myths have waited to be released from a *lisp* in
      time
To a mystery revealed beyond the mind!
How can there be a winged Messenger of the
      Mercurian Light
If there isn't the Power present to dispense
      involuntarily the gifts similar to a Christmas
      Light?

This is termed "the Race of Man." It is really a race of men. Every race has been modelled. You can see them in the museum in Chicago. They are all bronze statues with an ideal represented of the Race of Man, done by Melvina Hoffman. I saw them in about 1942. They are cast in bronze, waiting to be freed from a stereotyped, perfect figure into a vibrating, sonic intention.

Why is the sonic boom the topic? Because you fill the atmosphere with tones or sounds or the sonics of destruction by wrong language emotionalized instead of right language *glamorized!*

Your experience should be filled with glamour! It should be filled with elegance, for "All that I have is thine," and the glamour of God is seen in the stars that shine! Why would you doubt glamour? Because you have a dirt-filled mind? How glamour has been shunned because it is such an attraction to matter! No one wants you to be glamorous, you become too attractive. But is it the *matter* that is attractive?

Glamour is a concomitant of freedom; it is the evidence of the nullification of limitation. Even a scarf can give glamour to a robe of simplicity. A scarf can hold your attention, just as a rosary might hold your attention, on the healing effect of a proper color of your spectrum of light. There is no healing in a scarf! It is only in your attention to the color worn *as* the scarf — that attention opens a door to the frequency needed to free you.

Superstition is not understood. Superstition arises from an incomplete understanding of a symbol. The greatest superstition that exists is "you"! What do you wear as a result of it? The heaviness of a matter-world appearing as the stage for your need of cognition of the State. The moment you question, "Oh, why do I feel so terrible? Nobody loves me. I'm not wrapped in somebody's arms" — Wrap yourself in somebody's arms until you die, you will still die alone.

> I thought I had friends, I counted them many.
> So many days of life were spent.
> I thought I had friends and saw the wonder,
> Until "no friends" left a condition to ponder.
>
> I thought I saw friends, and then I saw none
> Were really free by being a legendary One.
> All were caught in the race of men,
> All caught in the bronze age of limited action and
>   allegiance.
>
> I saw friends, so declared in the language of time,
> All those three hundred or more I addressed with a
>   Christmas rhyme.
> Until I divorced myself from the realm of doubt,
> All the friends were there, and the envelopes
>   stamped with the Christmas rhyme of Love.
>
> But when it was announced that I was single again,
> It shocked all those friends who now would show
>   their allegiance plain.

One appeared, out of ten years so spent
Greeting friends, and then time said, "Where did
    they went?"

Do not count on people to be friends. Be One; find One
that is a friend. When you find *One* to be a friend, be One.
(It is a simple way to put it.)

I thought of friends along the way:
At one time it seemed that they were so glamorous
    and gay.
Then time corroded, demise appeared,
And the dimming of eyes was enhanced in the
    unreal.

The eyes no longer sparkled with joy,
The eyes of friends sometimes were *fiends* employed.
And thus we find it is wise to doubt
Those who say they are friends, when no love is
    radiating about.

But when Love is present, may Truth be found
Marching in rhythm on Earth, unbound.
But if you find those whom you love have dim eyes,
Be wary, because you cannot see with a clouded
    vision, without questioning, "What is your I?"

If a friend questions not what causes you to shine
And can put up with your declarations, watch out
    from behind.
Count on no man in the race of men.
Find only One and then see how it bends
Into time as a grace, and man starts to see
The face of loved ones appearing as HE.

Have you found a friend . . along the Way?
Be sure to tell them: "Straight ahead. *A droit!*
    It is the only way."

If they move to the right or they "gee" to the left,
The horse of the mind is not fully spent.

But if the gallop is grand and great,
You will know, the one riding the horse has no
        fate!
'Tis only to BE the invisible rider to time
That rides your horse, your horse of the mind!

When that horse is ridden,
May you find your groomsman a friend!

> **It is said that the great diamond of an
> unforgettable nature, for all of time, was the
> tear that Jesus shed; it caught the sunshine
> of His life.**

*What is the point of an alphabet from which you can make
your words if it is not to give them so many colors, all part
of a spectrum of the Unseen (by the eyes of time), the almost
opalescent spectrum of Light?*

What shines as "you" depends upon the state of your
mind for its density, its opaqueness, its translucence, or purity. It is not a state that is permanent; it is a state that you
have endured until a question is answered and you unearth
the glamour of a crystal-clear clarity. **If you do not want to
be clear, you will not be; and if you want to be clear and still
maintain your present pattern of thought, you will not be!
But if you do not *want* to be and just BE, tell me if the "I"
has been asserted.**

> **How do you know what it is like to be a
> Prince unless you attempt to enact the part?**

Try it and see where it leads you, for you will have the
force of intention behind your drama.

Language was never meant to bind you; it was given as a means to communicate an authentic cognition of indivisibility in the face of multiplicity and in the fun of appearing multiple and many.

This information is found and appealed unto by the other actors who appear ready for your directorship. If you cannot play the part, you will have to direct it in hell. If you enact the part voluntarily, you are naturally cognized as the director, for the Hall of Fame no longer bears an object of meaning for the past if it has no transcendent value for the Now.

The museum contains the relics of — a past glory? The museum contains the relics of a suggested warp due to being caught in time and space and the disintegrating force of conflicting forces. All that is left is that which could not speak. What is the characteristic of anything dead? There is no response to Life!

▼

Chapter VII

Harmonic Convergence

equality

education

brain/thinking

Temple of Beauty

harmony/rhythm

Soundless Eternality

Harmonic Convergence

We are overlooking the fields of seeding that has taken place as a result of our willingness to till the ground and prepare it. The furrows of concern and worry and the marks of dilemma are always brought to the foreground of our attention and frequently marked on the canvas called the face.

When men age, it is part of the decor of time. When men birth, it is part of the decor of time. When we are not a timed experience, we are a soundless eternality. So, if we are engaged in this scenario, embracing time and space and creating a dimension, we do so with the *intention* of experiencing. This experience is said to be relevant to everyone who speaks either the words of time or the Words that are like confetti from the mantle of Light.

The mind that is utilized and known by thought is there as an ingredient of our upbringing. As a result of our education, the mind is given such a place of worship that unless it is schooled to a large degree in logic on the subject under discussion, we feel that we are not as educated as we should be!

The thoughts utilized are "banked" as mind. How are you going to use this seeming organ and have it appear other than a "stop"? It is one thing to fill the bellows of an organ so it can speak as a mighty one; it is another thing to have an organ, such as the brain, and describe it as a mind. We now know that the brain is the organ; the mind is the schooled condition of the organ!

The great master organ that is piped with many ranks yields its tonality according to the ministrations of the one who registers it for performance, yields the tonalities commensurate to that which is to be performed, and comes alive under the disciplined approach of one schooled to wonder. So too does the mind and its inherent potential come forth in a new way under the authority which springs forth under the light of experience and intention. It speaks with assurance that there is Something beyond it and appears to be capable of realizing its own limitations, even when schooled to degrees.

A degreed mind usually bears witness to the amount of impediment. We are set loose on this surface planet to reveal the Solvent for the adamant nature of error. Error undetected runs loose as if it were a companion, and a needful companion, of the everyday world. There is nothing more erroneous than to think you have "a mind of your own." Everyone has got it, everyone is born with it, and *who did it?* It takes a great deal of *boring*.

We used to play hide and seek and say, "Bore a hole, bore a hole right in the sugar bowl. Who did it?" and then we would crack somebody in the back and run as fast as we could to hide. The game was that the first one caught became the one that got cracked on the back, but who ever thought of it as being a crack on the back?

How many of us get cracked on the back without realizing that we are playing a game so that others may hide and play seek with us. Some people will seek us and then hide from us, after they have given us a wallop and then asked to be detected for having done so.

It is an amazing level to which a child's innocent game becomes a nefarious action that goes on behind the backs of those who are supposedly geared to rescind the seeming mandate of error and allow the Solvent of grace and Love to be a living experience. This allows the ministrations upon the great, grand organ of the universe to once again be sounded with assurance, as the diapason of wonder and pitch is perceived by those who have audience in that great cathedral or the Temple of Beauty.

It is said that it was in the Temple of Beauty and Light that many were initiated into the rhythm that becomes essential in your worlds of to-morrow. The rhythm is essential because without it no melody of praise or significance can be anticipated. The surprise of Being can never be fully perceived, when it should be already known to be, and it *is,* by those who direct the Temple experience. *They are known, for they have been given to praise! They have been given to praise the Invisible, for they stand with the understanding, appearing to be expressed through words, while they remain under the Light yoke of fulfilling an interior mandate to see freedom expressed.* This can never be done without a melody, seeming to have words for those who need them, but wordless for those who sit and prepare to receive.

This does not mean that there is a void in the wordless realm; it means that there is no intrusion of thoughts. The mind has been stilled and quieted in order to receive the tonality that seems to be a force of stimulation in the vocabulary of the mind, a stimulation to look beyond the very bank of information that you have deemed to be your whole realm of existence.

If your mind is in question, do not be concerned! *If your mind is in question, it means you are becoming aware of the game you are playing. As soon as your mind is in question, you know I AM the Answer!* If your mind is not in question, you think "you" are the answer. "You" are the answer to what? The source of thought-propagation.

Thought-propagation is passed from one to another because the mind is a magnetic field which attracts thoughts. *You never create one of them!* The thoughts that you think are *never* your own; the thoughts that you think arise as a result of the One-thought bifurcated by a system contaminated and fettered by selfishness.

They say that selfishness is the root of all evil. It is not the root of all evil. There is no such thing as evil if men and women would stop looking in the mirror and would see *"Live!"* instead of "evil." The mirror always puts it backwards. L-i-v-e to you is the manifestation of life; in the mirror it is e-v-i-l. So, what you look at must not be considered evil; it must be considered the canvas which allows others to perceive the wisdom of wonder being portrayed on the visage prepared to receive information contrary to the thoughts of a contaminated field.

Any thought-field is contaminated when it mixes what IS with what *is not,* and, moreover, you do not perceive it. It is like most conversations. In the mornings, when I have to converse with people, it seems I have to take care of so much that *is not,* without saying what IS.

This is very important to perceive: As the mixture of thoughts continues, the adamantine nature of error continues to become denser and harder, and it takes a nuclear blast to create an opening. It used to be said that if there was a cleft in the rock, there was hope for the "I."[1] The rock was what you *thought* life was in the simplicity of a country style. In the sophisticated area of a city, however, it becomes sky-scraper-high with the cement of selfishness and hoarding, creating enterprise based on fear, need (which is naught), and division (when there isn't any)!

We say man is divided into races. Man is *not* divided into races; *men* divide men into races, cultures, and creeds in order to register within their ability the coloration of

---

1. "Rock of Ages, cleft for me, let me hide myself in Thee." (Augustus Montagne Toplady, "Rock of Ages")

speech to be utilized to satisfy those who demand that type of tonality engagement. The flute may appear to those who are of the myth of Pan, or the reed may appear, but the myth of the past is really just the myth of this present, gigantic colossus of mentality that is not imbued with the invisible Light. The invisible Light allows it to be seen as an imposter to the throne of man's divine attainment!

Divine attainment is nothing but the name given to everything that *is not* a "thing" but *thought* a "thing" until the *thing thought* is no longer thing-thought but Silence, perceived as fructifying, powerful, seeding, and bearing in blossoming — scent!

We know that every garden flower planted, if it is to bloom, will bloom. Lilies are now so co-ordinated with seasonal display that they have a time built in them to blossom. Just because they all show their leaves at the same time does not mean that they are all going to blossom, but God says, "They shall blossom, for I AM the wonder to their blooming!" That is the same with the seedlings called "you." You may not all blossom at the same time, but it is inevitable that you will because no word of Truth can be heard and not bear a blossom. How great or small the blossom depends upon what you have contributed to the richness of your experience by associating with those thought-patterns commensurate with an unlimited Source of inspiration, wonder, and the anticipation of a tyranny of Love that far transcends the stories of the past. If it were not for the immediacy and the nowness of this fact, I could not be saying it!

Do not expect to be with people who want you like they are! Be glamorous! Be the antithesis of everything spiritual! Be glamorous! Do not want any "thing." Go against spirituality. Do not *want* spirituality. Do not *want* sacredness. BE the sacredness, BE the living Spirit, BE the living glamour, BE the abundant nature of a wellspring!

What is the purpose of a harmony, a rhythm, and a melody? They must *converge!* If they do not converge, you do not have any ability for a composition. What is the world waiting for and has been waiting for, for years? **A harmonic convergence!** It seems impossible from the standpoint it is being offered, because those in the offering may not understand the *Gridwork* that goes into the convergence, which is calling upon the *artless nature of the inspired,* not upon the intellectual nature of the limited!

The limited nature of intellectuality reveals itself in extolling a condition. The unlimited nature extols the unlimited universe! Do you realize you make up the universe?! You have actually put the Milky Way out of your reach of wearing because you have confined yourself to such a surface impression. The cosmos is only given to those states of consideration that do not figure into your ken. Astrology is only given as an excuse for trying to study and incorporate what is beyond your reach into your "tree of life." Impossible!

An astrologer has about as much viability in your life as putting your life in the hand of stars. Most stars look at the sand! They are usually taken for movie impersonators, actors. You are told to look up to the stars because they are out of your reach! What if you were told to look at the stars in your midst and keep the cobwebs of belief from veiling your eyes of perception? Why don't you clear the cobwebs of your belief of being "this" (which you are not) and see a cosmic happening, harmony reigning as a convergence with the melody and the rhythm commensurate to the dance of the Unknown?!

> **How do you know the Unknown exists?**
> **It has a *rhythmic sway!***

The value of the future is in this fact: that it be relieved of being thought into the next number of years. The future is only the name given to those who persist in processive thinking instead of the verticalization of wonder! Wonder precludes process from appearing to impinge upon attainment. It is not process that gives you attainment; it is your unwillingness that gives process!

Protocol is essential because it is the manner in which you do something under the conditions that are pertinent to a specific way. There is a protocol in dealing with royalty. There used to be a protocol in dealing with dress. There is protocol in dealing with a secretary in an office. There is protocol in dealing with the boss of the office. There used to be! There isn't any more because everyone wants everyone equal, *in belief. Not really!* It is the mesmeric claim, it is the anesthetized condition, that makes you *think* everyone is equal.

You will *never* be equal through thinking. The only thing that is equal about thinking is the activity called "thinking." If you can say "I think," you are all equal in error! *I* do not think! The thought appears as a result of the unknown *I* that I AM! Ken Mills thinks, Jackie thinks, Kate thinks, Jo-Ann thinks, Mal thinks, David thinks. What is common is "think." Naming the "think" is what gives us the "-er": the think-er, the lov-er. It is the "-er" that makes the thinker.

Love is the liberator, and what can free but Truth? Mrs. Mary Baker Eddy said, "Love is the liberator."[2] Truth is the liberator; Mind is the liberator. [The sound of a truck's horn is heard.] I know you are there! We do not need you to sound! The object always makes a horrendous noise to announce its presence, even when it takes up the entire broad way!

It is the straight and narrow which leads to a correct pitch! This is why all people who wish to converge into a symphony orchestra in America pitch to the confines of A440. If you play that in Europe, you are out of pitch because there, I am told, it is A443. I am glad someone is counting

2. Mary Baker Eddy, *Science and Health with Key to the Scriptures* (Boston: Trustees Under the Will of Mary Baker G. Eddy, 1934), p. 225, line 22.

somewhere! The oboe is supposed to sound the pitch. You would wonder if they ever hear it in some orchestras!

How are people orchestrated? To make a living in a corporation called a symphony? To make a living in a corporation called an investment? A symphony appeared because everyone converged in music: in harmony, rhythm, melody, form. It was so gigantic in experience that there had to be a course given, called "music analysis" for mentalists. Musicians could understand it, but mentalists could not! They could only go into trance or float in and out of windows. A symphony orchestra was a convergence and *is* a convergence. Under a great conductor, what happens? Just standing and waving his fingers every now and then is not what is great; it is due to his age! The conductor should be evidencing what is inherent beyond the score, not a beat but movement! You can see what has happened.

You can say, "His look tells you." It does, but it is the movement which gets you beyond it. I give all kinds of signals for what The Star-Scape Singers are to do; sometimes one hand tells them what is coming and the other tells them where they are. They know this; the Polish choir[3] does not. This is the problem. Both choirs perceive, but one choir knows and the other does not know. They are all singers, but what is the difference? *Knowing what the movement means.* One is a signal for where you are; the other is a signal for what is coming. If you do not know where you are, you will not know what is coming; but if you know where you are, what is coming has already come, and thus is prepared.

What does this mean? For those who have expected the future, the Exemplar said, "I have come that ye may have life eternal." He could have said, "I AM here. There is no future, but because you do not know this, I have to say 'eternal' because eternity is the antithesis of anything that has to do with a time-space continuum."

---

3. Referring to a visiting choir that had been sponsored to come from Poland to rehearse with Mr. Mills.

If you are graced with questioning identity, the grace is really the prompting to look for the solution or the solvent to suggestion. It is so subtle and so simple that the educated cannot perceive the simplicity of the demand. The protocol demands you leave everything at the door of belief that is not becoming to the response, enter, and find that when you step through a suggestion — it never was! You used to have to stay in after school for thinking two and two is five. You were let out as soon as you knew it was four. The teacher said, "Thank goodness, it is four o'clock and I can get home early to-day." What blessed one blessed all! *When you once step through and perceive the solution to a configuration, the configuration is just an adornment.*

The Naka can be cast in iron, it can be cast in brass, and it can be cast in gold.[4] They are all different values, if you go by price, but they are not worth anything other than adornment of superficiality until you know what the Naka means. In essence, it means "the Center which embraces all." You know it is the Center because it is open and extending, with the full circle and the inner circle. The extension is never difficult when you radiate. Extension is only difficult when you think you have a point.

"Discussion" is a polite way of saying you can cuss at everyone else because they do not think as you do. That is why it is discussion, "dis-cussin'." It should be a distant relative (cousin) whom you hardly know! "To discuss" is a polite way of saying there is no agreement. That does not exist in a symphony orchestra; everyone *agrees* to go under the tension of A440. If you can tune an instrument by adjusting the tension, can you not attune the thought to where it is in pitch with the absolute demand of performance? What should play upon the strings? A bow!

Why is everyone so concerned when I mention anything that has a tremendous line of reference? I mention

---

4. The Naka is a Japanese symbol used as the logo of Mr. Kenneth G. Mills and his companies and shown on the spine of this publication.

food, and everyone starts to salivate. But when I mention divine, everyone becomes serious because there is so little thought that is equivalent. Why can you not talk about Love? There is so little thought about That which is Real. That *seems* to be the case. It is not.

One teacher said, "Perfection includes imperfection." That is wrong! It does not include imperfection; it *reveals* imperfection.

> *Truth* seems included within the mind; it reveals the mind-thoughts.
> *Love* is what allows you to exclaim when you have perceived the perception, or we say Love is that which allows us cognition. See?
> It is *Principle* that allows you to identify.
> It is *Spirit* that allows the dynamics of the cognition to live.
> It is *Soul* that allows the feeling to accompany the dynamics.
> *Life* is static; *Life-ing* is the registration of the Synonyms bearing relevance to the dynamics of the great organ of Light.

You can play on many manuals, but they are all pitched to a fundamental diapason. It is termed "the open diapason." For the higher tones to be balanced, you have a low bass thundering in an 8-foot stop, 16-foot stop, 32-foot stop. If your church is not large enough to hold a 32-foot stop, it is coupled with a sub-octave to create an octave lower. How often we create super-octaves and sub-octaves in order to give ourselves a greater colorful rendition!

People have said that black is so becoming. It is! Black is all colors absorbed. It is the reflection of — *no color?* It is a wonderful backdrop for *all color.* You cannot wear black well if you have not a spectrum of color on which to play the backdrop of your appearance. That spectrum of color becomes the backdrop of your appearance. Black may make you look slim. A diamond may let you appear to have a lot. But if in essence you are nothing but a selfish thought, your appearance is a selfish offering instead of a selfless offering. The wealthiest are those who are the most selfless, because they always receive. The selfish have no room to receive.

How can you *withhold* and have room for more? It is by your knowing "nothing" that others say you know something. They say, "There is a wellspring of unlimited inspiration which has nothing to do with the fluctuation of the rainfall of seasons." *How can you expect to see a harmonic convergence as a world experience if those appearing on the stage of drama refuse a Pitch that is set as a standard in order for each to play his part according to his achievement and the worthwhileness of his offering?!*

One of the most interesting bits of propaganda of the world to-day is that everyone is equal! We all are equal in that we evidence life, a body, and the attached head. The head is said to be the only part of the body that is empty and capable of holding what is termed "the brain." (The Egyptians "strawed-out" the brain through the nostrils at death.) It is an incredible gift to be used correctly. To use the information correctly sets you free from a mind that is disturbed by conflicting opinions.

Why is the Mind said to be divine and the brain said to be in time? Mind is aware only of What IS. The mind of time can appear to be aware of What IS and what *is not* at the same time. This is how the *Unfoldment*™ is being given this morning. My allegiance is to What IS known as "Mind," and that is why the other one you call "mind" is capable of functioning in your realm as sound engagement. Mind has never broken the Silence. *That is why Love in operation is effortless; your mind in operation is fatiguing!*

Why do you look so careworn? Why do you need pancake makeup? Because you are so much in your mind that your mind is wearing its compact out! Do not be so mind-full that there is no room in your compact for color. What is the purpose of fine makeup? It gives you what you should have naturally. Why is there a different makeup in performance? The makeup has to be exaggerated for distance in a large theater or it has to be subtle for a close-up camera that bears a magnifying lens. That is why makeup artists are very costly.

What makes a face glow?
Removing the one that *isn't*!

What makes the sagging rafters rise? Causing a rib cage to giggle. Why do rafters rise in a giggle? It causes an instant rhythm; you cannot cope with it, so *it has to have expression.* Laughter is nothing but convulsing to humor. Humor is so scarce, you do not know how to cope with it when it happens, so you laugh! In mind, in "brainology," there is no way of understanding what causes you to laugh. Laughter is a convulsion which happens under the pressure of seriousness and ridiculousness meeting!

Why can we not laugh at something that is not real? We should be able to, but it is difficult, isn't it, when you have a *mission,* when you have an intention that is clearly defined? Every Exemplar has said, "I will take on the infirmities of those whom I join, in order to elucidate the Point." For one who knows, this is only a temporary situation for *planing,* in other words, making the rough places plain.

When you have a clear intention, the variations that confront you are multitudinous and many, and frequently enigmatic. What are not acceptable are indolence, apathy, or a phlegmatic condition. An apathetic people is a conquered people, for their minds are so sedated that they do not perceive the energy of newness *before thought.*

"The air was so cold, the water seemed hot." We plunged in, knowing the *contradiction;* but having contradicted the suggestion, look at the *diction*. Conflict is always contra-diction; it is always *against speaking accurately*. When people contradict you, they go against what you are saying. If you are speaking Truth, most will contradict you. *They do not want to hear a new framework of sounds that causes them to question their acumen;* after all, they have been so schooled, they are erudite! There is no point to erudition ("your" edition!) if your edition is not new, with transparent covers. The only binding is the Truth!

What is the Truth?
That which you cannot contradict.

There is your contradiction. Truth is what cannot be "against statement"! "Contra-dict." Truth cannot be "against statement" because Truth does not know anything that is opposite; that is why it is not disturbed by contradiction. **Truth is not in the realm of being untrue.** *Truth is the force that allows the untrue to be perceived, as perfection allows the imperfection to be perceived, as the dying is perceived by the Life-ing, as the mindless by the Mind full of its own allness. You can tell when there is Soul present; if there is no feeling that embraces, Soul is not present, it is only a word.* If there is Love, it cannot be just a sound that does not allow *school* to be seen in a new framework.

How can you be led into a new station if you are heavy with satisfaction where you are?[5] A new position should give you a new chair, a new desk, a new garment, a new apparent mentality, and a new atmosphere. *You should not take anything of the old with you, other than the flowering of what your previous position offered. You should not refer to your old position unless it can bless the now.*

To move into a new position literally demands change. If you are going to fulfill a position in Toronto, it means that

---

5. The root meaning of the word "educate" is "out" + "to lead.".

you go from here to Toronto. You take everything that you have here with you, but you cannot take what is here with you. You cannot take this lodge; all you can take is the *fragrance* of the lodge, what you have gleaned from it! The buildings offer nothing, neither do the people, neither does the food. It is worthless if it is not exuding all that comes with a place of rest and seclusion. *As soon as a place becomes too large to welcome, it is too small for world considerations.* If a place is small and yet welcomes world considerations, it will grow, provided that welcome is present.

How is a welcome present?
By extension.

Who extends?
One who prepares without being asked what will be needed before one knows what is needed.
That is what a welcome is.

What is service?
That which is provided before it is asked.

What is wealth?
Wealth is that which is in use before it is necessary or called upon to manifest.

What is imagination?
That which has created in a limited way,
or That which is uncreated and is limitless?
One is redeemed and the other is errant.
The unredeemed has "this"
and "you" trying to change it;
the redeemed sees "this" as a play,
and the direction given.

It makes no difference whether you succeed or you do not, for it is already done! It is up to you: Are you going to take your time and prolong the belief or are you going to reduce it to its nothingness and allow the world, through *your* harmony and *your* rhythm and *your* melody, to be once again open to the possibilities of a truly harmonic convergence?

Man is a tonal experience — Man is a Song. He is *thought* to be organic. If he is *thought* to be organic and *known* to be a tonal experience, you are much more mind than matter! Isn't it amazing, the grace that allows what *isn't* to appear as "this" and still remain in its magical way? This is imagined as another day. If it were just another day, it would be like every other day. No day is the same as the day before, no moment is the same as the moment before, because every moment is a new creation. *Every moment, every second, is the time it takes for your newness to be perceived!*

▼

Chapter VIII

Midway Position: the Mute

sin/division

neutrality/mute

healing

invention

intention

constancy

tonality of Being

Midway Position: the Mute

[The recording engineer calls Mr. Mills' attention to a problem with his microphone.]

It was not fully on; it was on "mute." Is it not amazing how when a mechanical thing is not functioning, it is termed "mute" or "non-responsive." The condition of most: mute! Now we know a new name for it if it is not turned on — mute! Midway position: mute.

It is so interesting to consider the mute position as the position between "on" and "off." *The mute position is like the non-responsive position of those who are neither truly on nor truly off; they are the neutrals, you might say.* They are the ones who are partially present, and they are the ones who are really in a precarious position because the days termed "to-morrow" have no place for the situations where there is a non-definition of **intention**.

The mute position is almost like a state of separation: one is separated from responding from above or responding from below. It is, of course, a position observable as a result of the constancy of That which IS. You might term it "Energy," you might term it "Consciousness," or you might term it the "C/sea." The sea separates the continents. *The mute state separates; it exists but it does not provide.*

This was why invention had to take place. We invented the means of going onto the surface of the situation by providing canoes, the result of "Can you?" Can you see the need that developed? People incorporated and decided to work together to take an old log, hollow it out, and surface on the sea.

What have we tried to do with life? We have tried to make it worth living without ever having discovered the worth that is termed "living" or the worth that is termed "Life." To be evaluated from the standpoint of a neutral or a mute is impossible because we are in a state of *remission.* We are dormant and yet not dormant; there is the possibility and there is not the possibility.

> **What bridges are essential to-day**
> **to move over the sea of separation,**
> **of non-responsiveness?**

With *the tonality of Being*, we know that rhythm and melody provide us with a garment. With the condition of Being, it can be considered a tone: the tonality of Being. Without a tone being bridged, as Wagner pointed out, how under the sun can you ever expect an experience of extension? You cannot. "Knowing the tonality of Being" is an intellectual assertion without experience. When it is experienced, it is known to be rhythm plus melody and harmony; and then Life is known to be living, experienced.

If your life is devoid of living with rhythm and harmony and melody, then you know that there is a mute condition within you. You can usually tell a mute. A mute condition *never* extends. A mute condition is always entrenched in silence that is devoid of the support system of experience. *Experience experienced results in understanding.* You cannot give anything if you have not moved beyond the intellect, because *the intellect is mute.*

This is why it is stated that *you have to experience, otherwise understanding cannot be born.* All that can be born is another offering of an intellect. That offering is lifeless, because although it may have the words fitly joined together, it does not have the rhythm commensurate with Origin.

The origin of man has been the topic of many books. What has provided the material for all the books is the supposition that Man was created. **Man has never been created; men and women have been!** Man is the Light to the projection which you witness as your life unfolds, frequently without experience!

This is why *a society that rests with a sense of false satisfaction in the realm of surfacing-living, surfacing-life, is a society that is in abeyance for a moment and is being filled with dry rot.* This dry rot never shows until pressure is applied to it, and you find there is no sure footing upon which to stand. This is your intellectual scaffolding that should only be used for a short time! Otherwise it dry rots.

In our attempt to worship God, we forget that the God, to be worshipped, must be done so *out* of the mute condition. The mute condition means the instrument is present but not offering anything. It is costly, for it is an object of perception, as men and women are. *Unless men and women are out of the mute position and "on the bit," so to speak, there is no possible way for them, through the byte of an intellectual computer, to appropriate the Allness that is needed for those crying for a sustaining Principle.*

A melody can exist without words, but not without rhythm. There can be no art to living if the bridge is not erected, for *living is a tonal expression.* It is filled with the color of Presence and the color of perceiving your perception. You will perceive the perception that you are entertaining, finding it acceptable or unacceptable.

Nisargadatta was once asked by "a question mark" if he had ever met Ramana Maharshi, and he said, "No, but we are of the same State." The "question mark" said, "Do you think, if you met Ramana Maharshi, he would recognize you as the same State?" Nisargadatta said, "It would be impossible for him not to. It takes One to know One."

If you are still in doubt as to the paramount importance of *this* tonal framework for your reference's sake, then you had better realize that you are nowhere but in a valley that is mute. If you do not realize the universal significance of this offering on behalf of you, *for* you, then it will never become *as* you and bear the azure becoming one bearing the invisible cloak of devotion to the Ultimate.

You cannot conceive as a virgin if you have been contaminated by intercourse with false and sham teachings. A sham approach to life is one in which you are allowed to think that you are growing better and better, thinking better and better, and being better and better. It achieves nothing. It is only an attempt to steer an errant mind in a trough of an angry sea to the land beyond Nod, in spite of all your blinking!

No matter how much you flirt by winking at the tepid condition of most of time's people, you will still find the Truth steeped in the aroma becoming its utilization, as received in the Chalice or the Cup on a stand of reception. *You cannot receive if your cup is full.* You cannot understand the deadly nectar unless you have perceived it is the essential ingredient termed "Truth" that annihilates the foe in ambush.

Error is that which would have you filled with division. The root of sin is division. You cannot divide yourself from Deity, only in thinking you are separate — by *a decree?!* **Who has ever decreed that you are separate from your Maker,** other than an intellectual who is attempting *not* to define the Undefinable. Certainly the *defined* experience allows the Undefined to be perceived as existing.

You cannot expect a new birth if you have blocked the passage! You cannot expect a new birth and expect something just like "you" to come out. Who would want it? Who would want to go on creating like "you"? Would you want to go on creating like "you" to try to prove to yourself that Life continues in the form of a child? The child eventually buries you as the end of another epic in a belief system! Or would you rather consider *the child as that state of newness that is forever birthing, freed from the womb of an intellectual?*

Newness cannot be bred in the intellect;
the intellect can only try to define or limit it.

When I was a child, I thought as a child, with no limitations. I did not know why I could not fly! In one dream state, all I had to do was to think I could fly and I was flying over the neighbors' houses, off mountaintops, off roofs. I could not understand why everyone was looking *up* at me instead of beside me. All I had to do was imagine myself flying and I felt I was flying. Many others have had the same dream. By putting emphasis on that dream, we now have a means of flying. One is so costly and the other one so pristine!

Clarity does not exist any longer, even in our seas. *Our* seas/C's are all wrapped-up in so many different octaves or planes of energy that so many seas/C's are contaminated, so many sounding boards are cracked. What we need to tune an instrument is a pitchfork — a tuning fork! (A pitchfork is what you get for not using a *tuning* fork!)

A tuning fork is struck on a hard surface, then put to your temple so that you can give the pitch to your choir. It is fascinating, it is put to your *temple*. It is not put to your knee or to your ankle; it is put to your temple. It is not put to your chin; it is put to your temple. It is in the Temple that the real offering has to take place. *The Temple is that construct of your imagination that you set aside as sacred or separate from the mass of thought-considerations.*

There is nothing wrong with the mind; there is nothing right with the mind! It behaves perfectly well according to what you feed it. You utilize the thoughts that are in keeping with your ideal or your hero or your model of excellence, and the thoughts appear that support it, but you cannot mar or blur your model by having other considerations about it.

You can never have a drawing of an invention if you have not seen it before it is drawn. How many attempt to have a drawing of an invention before it has been seen? How do you know that what you are seeing is the drawing of your intention? (What you are seeing as *your* experience, not mine!)

> **If your experience of invention**
> **is not drawing attention**
> **by its natural, all-inclusive extension,**
> **you have not experienced a clear definition.**

How can you draw upon resources that you have not defined? How can you draw upon a tone quality when there has not been an example? How can you call upon the Unknown and know it as an example if you have not a clear intention? *There is one mark, and that is* **constancy;** the one mark of a sophisticated mute is inconstancy.

When fluctuation is in your life, you had better consider moving *your* button on your transmitter to "on." The red light is "on," which means "Everyone else stop!" for what you are hearing puts an end to the traffic of the mind, but allows the vehicle to pass when you perceive the verdant nature of newness (green). *You cannot remain in the amber light position.* It is energized on both sides and immediately warns you that there is to be a change in flow. Lights give you warning in order to allow flow.

People on the highway of time, in mechanical vehicles of the mind, need direction in flow, otherwise they would create a jammed grid. Why do you persist in thinking you have a right to flow in any direction you wish (unless you have the green light)? The red light means you have to stop and consider the danger involved in going through with your intention with only a partial presence. When men and women start to flow in keeping with a grid of energy, they will not need the obstructions called bodies. They will not need to be "enhoused" in steel or plastic (cars) to move around. I have moved without the body or the vehicle of a car and visited other areas, in the twinkling of an eye, and have had it verified in its very nature.

It does absolutely no good if you are a levitator! What is the value of thinking you have altered the gravitational field of "you," if you have not proved by your life that *the only gravity is false identity?!* The value of levitation is to know the spirit of levity! With a suggestion of heaviness, it takes an intellectual persuasion to make you realize that your rational, logical mind has a next-door neighbor — paranoia!

Who can ever tap the wonders of the "go" position, while still retaining a foothold on the position of "mute"?! One writer pointed out how so many people say, "*This* is my life! *It is the most important thing in my life. I will pretend to give everything to it, but I will hold back a little bit (quite a lot really) in case it does not come through as it is supposed to, and I do not get enough fine praise in the media. I will hold back just to make sure I have got enough left in case this whole thing collapses.*"

"This" is bound to collapse! What will remain is the intrinsic worth of an artistic, Tonal persuasion, captured so that others will know it happened. What is a Wagner if his great compositions were not recorded symbolically as a happening? But try to play Wagner without knowing his attainment *spiritually* (as they say)! What would be the music without a conductor who knew the Standpoint from which Wagner received the inspiration and could wonder at his achievement? For he was able to put into a symbolic form that which was delineated as a *Tonal encounter.* You might say these lectures are this.

Why are you important? Because unless you have studied and accepted the Source of inspiration, how can you direct anyone interpretatively into the realm of tonal, heavenly experience?! **Earth is Heaven; it is due to atonality that it is hell! All heavenly experience is fecund with rhythmic, harmonic, melodic intent!**

People will not understand what you are saying if you have not experienced beyond your intellect. If you have not experienced but are in the activity of experiencing, then your words may still bear the mark of understanding, which can mark a line for others to follow.

It is not *understanding* that frees anyone new, because there is no one new. It is a radical stand you have to take (*you* have to take; *I* do not), because the mind utilized as servant behaves as one. This is the living evidence of it. *You* are the living evidence of it! *You are getting out of your life exactly the clarity you are putting into it* as a result of your intellectual accumulation. As you appear to grow "in age," they say (in order to try to understand *process*), you are acquiring more and more intellectual considerations to be filed in your system.

Your mind is a gigantic computer, *totally indiscriminate*. That is why a child needs to be guided. The mind is totally indiscriminate. After a very young age (I think it is four or five), the child starts to lose the clarity of his own inventiveness and starts to take on the restrictions of the situations surrounding him. Clarity must be evidenced by the parents in the ideas of "Do unto others as you would have them do unto you," or "Be kind to that animal because that animal is your friend." If the child is not told the animal is his friend, he can kick it, throw it out, and when he is older, the parents will go with it!

Children have to be taught the way in which they shall go. For the propagandized populace to think there is any hope for the world without the children being properly educated and disciplined is a mute state. There is absolutely *no hope* because the leaders of the world have become totally unselective in their thought-force. They only select what will do the most good for the seeming *objective society*.

Fundamentalists are really those who know that the allness of God is more than a concept; it is a *living experience of Love with no discrimination*. This does not mean that you cannot tell clean water from infected water; it does mean that you do not drink it. That is all. You do not say it is good or bad; you just say, *"Do not drink!"* The shams today would have you drinking a little bit of this and a little bit of that, and then wondering why you have not achieved anything. People may wonder why *you* have not achieved much; perhaps they do not realize that you *have* achieved a lot, but due to your mentality you have *refused* to allow it to appear in your inventions!

Just having a lot of ideas running around in your head and trying to put them into action is *not* inventiveness!

> Inventiveness happens in the seclusion and
>   the stillness
> When the still, gigantic Voice, unheard in
>   time,
> Pops *the latch of your coffin mind!*

There is not one thought that you think that will do you one bit of good if it is not filled with love and the expectation and the knowingness of a divine cause! It will not be *directed for the right purpose.*

> **What is the right purpose?**
> **To set the captive free from the belief of**
> **sickness, sin, and death.**

A healing does not only point to the presence of God; it points to the lessening power of material suggestion! In God's kingdom in the Light, in the Energy that IS, there is nothing to heal! When you realize that in essence you are divine energy (not material, *"no-thing"*), then is it surprising that perfection or healing takes place?

Inspiration without intention, without
architecture, and without invigorating the
drama of precipitation, bears little evidence
of the divine agenda.

*Everyone in this room should be so filled with newness
and invention that every encounter with what seems to be
yesterday or to-morrow is invigorated by destroying any
robe of limitation.*

Music should be setting people free; it should not be an
entertainment. This is why the symphony halls of to-morrow
will be therapeutic in intention. *The musicians of the future
will bear* **Tonal persuasion** *reverberating through the crys-
talline platform upon which one stands and finds* **the vibratory frequency commensurate to emancipated Being.**

You who go around, parading in skulls and spending all
kinds of money on having your hair done, face done, body
done, clothes done, have some concept of the cost of being
in fashion. You are so aware of fashion! It is one of the most
remunerated professions, along with doctors. *If you know
the cost of staying in fashion, why would you think it is so
cheap to don a new garment?* If this one costs you so much
to keep clothed all these years of your life, *can you imagine
the cost of putting on new robes of Righteousness?* It means
it sets you apart from everything that looks like "you"!

Why do you think so much about your scales? You are
constantly *weighing* . . the matter, when you would like to
see less of it. But what is seeing what? *Are you seeing your
Model, or are you trying to ape it and thus having all the
hoariness that goes with imitation and not the eternal vigor
of a pristine conception?*

It is "fun to be fundamental" as long as the mental is
trained to utilize the tonal language of communication and
you find **the tonal language bearing reference unto the divine
tuning fork of Oneness.** *The tuning fork is always two*

pronged, but the Tone is given by One. It is not the two prongs you put to your temple.

That is what has happened. A pitch appears divided by the line of attention directed from me to you, and you bow upon it according to your innate demands for "Music, Sahib!" The body of the instrument magnifies the sound. Why are all the modern bands so noisy? There is no message. *The noise is sedating all the thousands of people in a cataract of cacophony,* because they do not have the disciplined education of what music *is* even in analysis.

From grade one, we were taught how to sing, and then how to read as a class, and how to sight-read as a class, and then how to offer as a class. Each activity marked less and less of the individual and appeared as a harmonic experience within the class. What was not of consequence was erased on our slates; we did not use video screens!

*You have to know what it is like to use a **felt** eraser.* Today there is no feeling, there is only pressing a button to remove the information from a screen. When you had to clean the blackboard for the teacher, you did it with a piece of felt as an eraser and it was because *you wanted to do it.* The *feeling* was present. What was of no use was no longer on that black surface, and *the chalk marks of yesterday gave the unmanifested surface a chance to give you courage for what appeared as your next session with your divine instruction.*

The board, to be really clean, was washed. You did not find a pure white surface, you found a glistening black one. It is out of the unmanifested that the tendencies of invention reveal themselves, even in the formation of a number one. It took so long to realize: there could not have been the figure *1* without the Unknown appearing symbolized as a *0*. It is too bad the *X* became the unknown; it is the *0* that is really unknown. It holds the secret: for it to be a *0*, there has to be a center! To be an *X*, it is obvious. That is why an *X* does not mark a mystery anymore; it is what is missing in the *0* that has to be found! That allows you to bridge what is known to what is not known!

When you have visited these strange lands and strange peoples, then you start to perceive that even the Sea/C with its uncharted course was there because of the Energy appearing as tonal consciousness, available as awareness and, unto the mind, as perception. That is why Consciousness-Awareness-Perception is available. Perceiving all this, can you say, "I have not fallen for this screenplay, for the Light has gone up in my inner audience chamber and I know that the divine Light of Consciousness has revealed, upon my screen of awareness, this many-figured action in order to allow others, who attend unto our performance, to perceive, through the attention chamber, the visual aspect of freedom."

How many of you are allowing the words to appear to enhance your dark glass of intellectuality instead of allowing them to make the intellect a servant of your highest intentions?

How many in this room put This first? Just ask yourselves. "Put what first?" The Truth of Being authentic first. Naturally you would be here.

> **Where else can you go and be cognized?!**
> **Anywhere else, you appear like everyone**
> **else. Here, you are known to be an extra**
> **special parcel unto time.**

You did not come Federal Express, and it was not overnight service! It could have been *instantaneous!* Unfortunately it has been years of posting. When are your vows ever going to be taken in the Real marriage? *How you vow to serve your pocketbooks and the things that are passing, and refuse to accept the unlimited cache of your divine inheritance already stored and ready for you! It is all available when you request it **All** and assume **the responsibility** and the response to the ability.*

There is no point to being a prophet of gentle persuasion or gigantic persuasion! *You cannot persuade a computer to smell the apple blossom!* You do not try to persuade a mechanical contrivance to enjoy what is not a mechanical contrivance, but you certainly can allow it to indite a message of wonder so that your intellect does not stand in the way of your wonder at the blossom of an apple and the penetration of its substance, to reveal the invisible orchard offered to those who have tilled the soil and prepared for the seeding of eternity!

Thank you.

[Mr. Mills eats some blueberries.] Is a blueberry not wondrous? It is no wonder to you at all if you have not seen them. When they first appear, they are dark green. Then they turn pure white, and then they gradually turn blue. When the leaves are ready to give up their fruit, they turn red. They fire the blue of devotion (the blueberries) so that you may imbibe the only berries that contain the enzyme myrtillin. I wonder at a blueberry as the gown of such uniqueness that it was created, in all the multitude of creations, to bear the only enzyme known to be born by any fruit that we take unto our table. **What is the Enzyme of your life?** *The blueberry has no intellect, but it knew enough to be the custodian of myrtillin, the sacred fruit of Venus, the planet of Love.*

▼

Chapter IX

The Plane of Reconciliation

recovery/discovery

world/five senses

art

music

intuition/insight

Invisible

Identity

The Plane of Reconciliation

We are approaching you from that plane termed "the Plane of Reconciliation."[1] It is the Plane whereby We are inviting all who are within the range of this tonality to conceive the possibilities that are present in the bridgework of this sonic embrace, for it allows the Invisible and the visible to be reconciled.

It is within the encoding of everyone who hears this to respond within the section of their attunement to that aspect that is considered one of the Synonyms of the divine.

We are all called upon to pitch woo/*wu*, not "why"/*wei*.[2] We are all called upon to pitch Love, woo. We are all called to be upon the stage called Earth, because we have chosen to be part of the cast that is capable of exemplifying, for those in audience to see the job that is being done as the Earth is being prepared to turn on its axis and be given back to the pristine state of conceptual beauty.

---

1. "'We' always points to the all-inclusive nature used by royalty and is always considered a grace, for it is a divine all-inclusiveness, thus capitalized and set apart in the lectures, pointing to the impersonal Nature and its all-encompassing activity." — K. G. Mills

2. *Wu-wei:* "This controversial Taoist term has the literal meaning of 'non-doing' or 'non-striving' or 'not making.'" Philip Kapleau, *The Three Pillars of Zen* (New York: Anchor Books, 1980), p. 384.

Beauty may be caught in the mirage of art, but the Truth of Being is also *behind* and *beyond* the brushwork of the artist. *Any art that breaks the mirage is always under the stroke of the divine.* So it is that in the sequestered spot of your deepest considerations, We have asked "the angels"[3] who attend unto you to precipitate unto your pools of receptivity those forces that will enhance the spiritual pockets of your eternal cache.

You cannot go on identifying primarily with your objective confinement. You must understand that you can never offer understanding unless, through the renunciation of your belief system, you have experienced what it means to be considered one of the holy Ones of God.

What are the holy Ones of God? Those are the unnumbered Ones who have rescinded the false identification and have sounded forth in the proclamation of the divinity possible as Life living abundantly, freed from the adjudications of biased and contemptuous thought. All those who have assumed the name of the Called are those who are endowed with a Soul pitch from Home base! All those who have perceived the Pitcher on the mound know that the great ball of Light was given as a symbol of the world to be passed from generation unto generation until it was restored as a gem in the crown of our conceptual might.

We have dreamed and are continuing to dream a fantasy! We have dreamed not only a jungle fantasy,[4] we have dreamed an asphalt fantasy and a corporate fantasy. We have dreamed a fantasy all supported by the forms called human beings, parading in a computered-like way to fulfill the mandates of a struggling ignorance. Instead, they should be renunciates, in other words, *given to Light,* walking the hallways and by-ways of any structure, shedding light upon the suggested shadows of incompleteness.

---

3. "Angels: the power of the Invisible activity symbolized, and being available in the lives of men and women." — K. G. Mills

4. "Jungle Fantasy," the title of a painting (acrylic on canvas) by Kenneth G. Mills.

You who are attuned to the feeling world, the sensorial world, know very well that the senses can never indite a correct message. You know that even color affects the taste you have for food, but as you have perceived, in the color of food rests not the taste — rests not even *the color! Color is a mirage!* It is a fantasy! *The art of the Work is the artlessness of the Invisible appearing visible. It causes a re-orientation to the **perceptual** might of the human and beckons and invites an open **conception**, as we have perceived that on the mound of the Pitcher stood the cross of an Exemplar.*

The bases have to be covered, because every dealing we have has to be squared to Earth. Every strike we make is not to win the game, it is to show that rules and regulations are only supportive of accurate movement. It has been said that "from sense to Soul my pathway lies." How many have perceived the lies that have confused and confounded those who were assembling their forces of cognition in order to be adopted and adapted by that very force of inspired might that would bring about a conciliation — but not a concilia-tion between the senses! The five-sense world can never be reconciled to the Invisible. But you do have within your five-sense world the penetrating force of two other oppor-tunities; they are unlimited and they allow a reconciliation of the Invisible and the visible to be perceived as an actual-ity termed "authentic": the development, the unearthing, of *intuition* and *insight!*

Intuition always seems to come before insight, for you do not perceive insight without intuition, which *beckons one to come inside* and acknowledge the attribute of won-der, a handmaiden of insight.

We cannot go on dealing the various cards of a prob-lematic game of life. We cannot go on trying to find an answer in this computered age, which in so many areas lacks the curiosity even of an avalanche, even of an eruption, even of a volcano, even of a revolution. Who is really excited or interested? Only those who make arms, only those who make substance some *thing,* only those who think in terms of numbers, only those who have forgotten.

How many are realizing that the Magi may be claiming freedom from reading stars of lesser accomplishments?

You are not for sale; you cannot be sold in the backyard as antiques or useless pieces of humanity in a public yard sale. *How many of you sell yourselves to time and forget to bear the Timeless?* How can you reconcile yourself to a position in any corporation, or in any activity, and suffer the lies of identity? You cannot! *You were not made for the purpose of deception.* **You were made to allow others to see in your performance how a moving, rhythmical vessel or a divine idea could appear as a conception walking!**

This is the only way that conception can be unconfined. It cannot be contaminated by the theoretical and the logical arguments of intellectual neighborhoods. People gather together in order to console each other in their limitations, instead of gathering together to count the blessings that have been bestowed upon a movement of parts fitly joined together, termed "a body" of incredible magnificence and wonder: God's gift to man!

Why should we leave it as a bronze statue by Melvina Hoffman in the Hall of Man in a Chicago museum? The statue does not talk, the statue does not walk; it is a symbol waiting to be freed from a metallic state, which is below the lowest state that you can fall to in order to evade the wonders — even lower than the animal, vegetable, and mineral kingdoms.

To see something cast in bronze, it is well to have known the living model, because by knowing the living model, the bronze is freed to move beyond its solidarity.

What is the task force of to-day? It is not being trained in military warfare of the visible enemy. *The task force of to-day deals with perceiving the hidden enemy of thought-forms that attempt to invade your planes of Light and attempt to be adopted as if they were part of your thought-field of discipleship. Thought-forms which are penetrating your cache of possibilities must always conform to the Diapason that you have accepted for your very foundation of the great organ to be used in an anthem of praise.*

You cannot use just mixtures, because mixtures on the great organ can never be satisfying, unless a tonality of fundamentality is perceived and the mixture adds what we might call a glistening tonality to a totally all-encompassing sound. It gives you another spectrum or plane of titillation.

The magic of music is that it comes from a composition that has been limited to time and to the timber of our forests (manuscripts) and translated via the objects of suggestion into a tonal framework of reference which has an appeal. *You cannot copy the experience of inspiration.* It is not even in the baton of the conductor, but the conductor annihilates the impoverishment of egoism that is in most performers. If he is a great conductor, he allows the music to have wings and fly on the plane of offering a dispensation of an angelic wonder of rapture.

"Music" is such a word, such a constellation! It is like an experienceable Milky Way of tonality! You might say, music is a scintillating experience of the Milky Way, possible to all those who have ears to hear. What inspiration drops upon their span of attention!

What you sow in attention you will reap in wonder!

What is more full of wonder than all the limitations of the object being given to vibrations that appeal to those attuned to the *Pitch of universal significance.* You are tonally pitched!

If this lecture is transcribed and read, it will be difficult to penetrate if you utilize all the senses instead of that which is beyond them. It will, as a transcribed lecture, give you *procedure* in the operation of to-day's world; it will not give you the *exit!* If this were in process and needing to be transcribed before hearing, it would not be under the aegis of what is termed "the Invisible," and thus manifested by a voice in order to be heard and to be captured on a magnetic-field!

You treat it with such commonality that you suffer the disease of the common, ordinary, mass-man. Those who are attuned to a pitch of concert performance should attune themselves to the rendition of an authentic Score and not one contaminated by bias and contemptuousness.

Contempt arises in the mass because That which does not depend upon temptation has a power to penetrate those who do not wish to be tempted, and their refusal is called "contempt." It is with time they are imbued and will die in the ignorance of their contemptuous attitude towards the emancipated Synonyms for Reality and *of* Reality.

If you, in the by-ways of time, do not consider in depth the inherent Force that *allows* your presentation, then you are in a scenario of rejecting the possibilities of emancipation from your belief system. You will die and awaken with *the same structure as the one you left!* People do not inherit other bodies freed from where they left off; they *go on* where they left off!

Why? Because Woo, Love's Pitch, was not accepted. "You must make woo," we used to say when we used to "neck" with what appeared to be a new-found love. We used to "pitch woo." To-day they do not want to take the time! They just want to enter with no obligation into an attempt of oneness without losing any freedom. *Impossible!*

Force demands responsibility, and that demand of responsibility is sincerity and fidelity to Principle and to purpose. You do this as part of the cast on the stage called the Earth while those in audience attend unto your transformatory presentation, for you are revealing an invisible

Script, indelibly written upon your Scrolls which are now perceptible in the light of intuition, not in the light of your five senses. *In the light of intuition, you no longer believe, you* **know** *that you are one of the stars in order for the Milky Way to sparkle in the constellation of your thought-patterns which point to a cosmic wonder.*

You can say, "This is the most impractical lecture I have ever heard!" *It is!* It has nothing to do with practicality; it has to do with the *dance*. It tests your mental achievement to see what thought-forms and what thought-patterns attempt to interfere with an unearthly consideration! It tempts your thought-patterns to re-dress in the garment becoming inspiration. Inspiration springs from "inspire," and that which is inspired is discovered, and that which is discovered was *never* in the discovery. As soon as a thing is discovered, it is a symbol. That is why Truth is a discovery. You cannot have a symbol for Truth, other than the alphabet. But the alphabet of sound reveals the tonality of the non-symbolic nature of Truth.

> *Truth* is *discovery!*
> **Listen!** *Truth* is *discovery!*

When you discover you are not this blob of flesh,
    Truth is the discovery!
When you realize you are not this singer,
    Truth is the discovery!
When you realize you are not this speaker,
    Truth is the discovery!
When you realize that you are not this thought,
    Truth is the discovery!
When you realize you are not this tonality,
    Truth is the discovery,
Either you would not have the courage
    to find the discovered so insubstantial
    and yet substantial.
What a reconciliation of the Invisible and the visible!

It is so simple . . in discovery; it is so complex in the discovered. Look how you have to work to support the discovered, because you *refuse to recover* from false identity! You refuse to recover from false identity. This is why the discovered is so difficult . . to maintain, to support, to enhance. As long as you think "you" have to support what others are going to discover as "you," you are creating a need, which means something is lacking.

Need always suggests lack. The only time you may say you need is when you know you do not need, and then it is only for the stage performance as a prop. Then others will be convinced of the unlimited nature of imagination and fantasy and enabled to precipitate what will satisfy the doubt, until they find themselves no longer a doubter but an awareness of a spontaneous conception. It is so simple!

You cannot say, "I will love this one; I will not love that one." You enact a part to allow others to open the Heart. What does the Heart open one unto? To the wonder of what appears and to the feeling of unity. It has nothing to do with age, it is obvious. The wonder of virgin Love is amazing grace! It is the only State that can realize and see what IS with insight. That which is not a virgin State sees options. That which is not a virgin State sees doubt, sees ways of creating detours and trying in its vanity to have company on its way.

How often has history recorded the extra-ordinary? Seldom in history books, because it points to the destruction of history. It is usually written about as a situation in *hindsight*. It was *foresight* that allowed a doubter to perceive the doubtless condition of a pristine, authentic Nature, but having been impure, it was unable to relate to it other than with hindsight. With hindsight you see how you have negated foresight, while insight has been promised. **"Before ye call, I have already answered!"** refutes the sense of tense, time, and space and allows you the incredible experience of being endowed with what is termed "the Ultimate."

The God-Source goes by so many names until experienced. You have to use them as you use the notes to play on a keyboard. What is released when you release the damper from the strings is a Tone that has nothing to do with steel, ivory, lead, or wood! It has only to do with the inherent heart of the instrument, the sounding board. It cannot be cracked with the insanity that parades to-day and calls itself sane.

Why do you go on waiting for despair and disease to cause you to consider forfeiting a false identity? Why do you not see what has been pitched from the Hill of Golgotha by the greatest Exemplar we have close to us to-day, termed "Jesus of Nazareth"? But guess what the gossips said? "Who ever heard of anything good coming out of Nazareth?"

It is not the good coming out from any *place;* that is where *hindsight* has to describe what was right before the eyes of the people. Fear and bias and prejudice said, "This is a threat to our power." If people are not properly educated with a set of principles, the mandate to be lawful, forgiving, and kind cannot be enacted because no one knows what it means! It is a good beginning. You are supposed to study, and if you do not, the law is the hickory stick! If you are not kind, the law is rejection . . and you *feel* it! And when you *are* kind, it is what? A reconciliation!

This is why, if you are educated properly, you are kind even to those who have slandered you, because there is no hope for *that* state of thought. You offer that very situation a possibility of reconciliation. There is none other than you fulfilling your Mission, regardless of the hell and the agony of it. Whatever the ecstasy is, it is beyond any mental configuration. It is just "doing the job" for which you were called!

Most people retire at sixty or sixty-five, and people are being asked to retire, with a slight reduction in their payoff, at an earlier age because there are not the funds. There is not the substance to support a staff of teachers or a staff of workers, for it is not "business as usual." Why is business not as usual? The business that IS is really penetrating the spheres of false activity and causing people to consider, what *are* they *doing?*

A *depression* is not the state of this country or of this world. That is the way the unenlightened describe it. There is no such thing as a depression, only in the valleys of decision and in the canyons of doubt where some people try to holiday and (provided they are carried in a carriage!) chase a ball over a course — of grass. Grass is a symbol of the passing, the insubstantial!

What is the point of having a "club" if it is not used on you when you need it?! It is obvious from the lack of love, discernment, and wisdom in public affairs that there have been few occasions where *obedience* has been really felt. Clever intellectual manipulation has taken its place.

The fields in Europe are so promising in the spring and early summer. They are covered with this incredible yellow-golden glow of colsa for hundreds and hundreds of acres. In the spring in Italy the hills are covered with a golden glow: genestri. Why is it that we see golden glow on our hills here, in our fields, and we look at it without wonder? Can you imagine the amount of paint it took to do all those flowers? Can you imagine the fairies at work pressing the tubes of paint so that your *angels of expectation could brushstroke the fruitage of a seed?*

Why do you allow your imagination to be so confined to objectivity that you cannot move in this Realm? For you see this Realm not! You know it *is* because of what you hear, and you know that if it can be said to you, it is because it is only possible when you have a clearly defined intention about "the job."

The job is never defined; *it is already done!* But what do you do? You *attack* life instead of *allow* living to manifest itself as you volunteer to play the voluntaries necessary for the worship of the Invisible!

All temple service is the result of giving oneself to the service of the Invisible, in spite of the talk about how to keep the visible filled with people and money so the temple will not fall down and will still be a tourist attraction! People visit Chartres because of its inherent mystical splendor. In some way you cognize, as soon as you walk through its portals, that this bears significance, for you have passed through a maze of byways and highways of life just to get there. But what is this maze upon the floor of this cathedral, if you did not have to take the bull-like, obstinate intellectual nature and make it realize there was no freedom from that maze without the linen thread of the unknotted Light of wonder!

You cannot enter such a cathedral with such proportions and *feel* what it is if you relinquish the Mound, for it is from the Mound of translation and transfiguration that you start to perceive what is hidden beyond the sight of those who are just tourists inspecting a so-called "place to be seen." It is the new type of social thing to do. It used to be that the place to be seen was at the Vanderbilts, the place to be seen was at the Rockefellers. To-day, since everyone seems to be "a tourist," the places to be seen are Chartres and Mont Saint-Michel.

The whole purpose of visiting a place of wonder is not *to be seen,* it is *to see,* because if you do not see you do not know enough to listen. If you do not know enough to listen, you do not know what can be *heard.* For they were never meant to house other than those in need on their pilgrimages — from sense to Soul — even through the belief of Crusades. Every system has its followers until it is known to be beyond the filing system of the mind, its computer, and its bytes, and that system reveals that the lost treasury of to-day is found in the simplicity of Being.

There is no good or bad, right or wrong. The Guide would give you the line: Whatever you do, is it causing the Pitch enabling one to be part of the symphony of Soul? Are you creating enough tension on the strings of your life to allow your Heart to respond when someone lifts "the felt" of suggestion by asking, "What is it that makes you so different, yet so wonderful and so attractive? You are vital and dynamic. You have not said very much as yet, but I know you have approached the hem of the garment woven from the one linen thread of constancy. Speak and tell me your pitch of woo, so I may be embraced in the crocheting work of Light. I must crochet for time a mantle of warmth until I don the scintillating tonal pattern commensurate with the Milky Way."

The Milk has become so far beyond your reach because you need the Meat of the Word; you are no longer sucklings! Do not behave as if you have a rented vehicle! Yours is *charged* with an intention, and some have called it a destiny, to be the living evidence of a coincidence between the human and the divine, since you have reconciled the visible and the Invisible.

For this We are truly grateful, and for these words that have fallen from the cornucopia of plenty into the tonal framework of your Heart's reception. To this we give acknowledgment and due praise, for in That, Principle is raised and the Light of eternality shines upon us, one and all!

▼

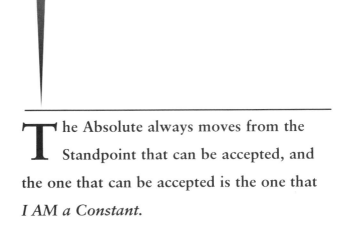

T he Absolute always moves from the
   Standpoint that can be accepted, and
the one that can be accepted is the one that
I AM a Constant.

Chapter X

A Fool's Utterance?

dark forces

healing/health

language/voice

imagination

Silence

The Word

A Fool's Utterance?

Where is the fool?
One who is bound to what isn't,
and thinks it good.

A Fool's utterance? **A Fool is one who can disengage the logic of the intellectual mind.**

We have been listening to the utterances of Fools who have appeared to walk o'er the pages of time and be transmitted as a viability through the symbol of the word, which seems to satisfy the intellect that they passed this way. Certainly, the movement from sense to Non-sense has been elucidated by many words and by many lecturers who have pointed over and over again to what you already know, that words should lead you to where no words *are*. (That does not mean what you *think* it means.)

When a word ceases to be a word, it is a living force of change! You will know when your words are more than words, for each one that is uttered from the wellspring of Being will bring a natural change, not from oldness to newness but from solitary confinement in supposition to the light of an emancipated State where the door is open and the light of infinite possibilities may be symbolically described as being present.

We sit here and with attention listen to these words. You have been given many questions to consider in depth. Why "in depth"? Because most of your life experience is rooted to the thought-patterns that instill within you a superficial feeling of togetherness when there is nothing but separateness. It seems this way in what even appears as your families. If you look to the root system, it is evident that very few use the taproot to extend deeply into the refreshing waters that bring about a harvest.

The grapefruit tree, grown in certain soils, always has "a taste". . that *you* give unto it. But there are those grapefruit trees that tap the richness of the soil at such a depth that they take unto themselves the mineral content of the earth which, as it is, is entirely unutilizable by you. The trees have given their life to helping to modulate energy into a *pattern of acceptance.*

The pattern of nature is such that it is adorable — as are the wee folk! They are all there through our imagination. Those of a scientific bent will always tell you, in their bent position, that leprechauns and wee folk do not exist. Of course, they do, if you *want* them to exist! Of course, you can see them if you *want* to see them. You see me, do you not?

Students) Yes, Sir.

Then how bent are you? I am more than "me"! But if you can imagine me a wee folk, you can see how skilled is your imagination.

We have the ability to project such an incredible fantasy, all in the realm where it seems so substantial because it appears dimensionalized. As soon as anything bears a dimension, especially the one you are in, it seems to have a viability that is impressive, and that impressive viability becomes *oppressive* to the artist's Soul. When forced to accept the seeming because of its impressiveness, the artist tries to get at this impression and tries to find what is at the root of this impressiveness.

The Impressionists have tried to do away with the stimulation of the objective sense and reduce the impressive to an impression. This impression by the great Impressionists carries a mark of another dimension, but due to your incredible ability in imagination, the impression becomes a three-dimensional expression clothed in a spiritual garment. This is why impressionism is so easy to accept, because it does not demand that you take the object; it demands that you be open to receiving what is present when the object is less defined.

The intellect has to be sidetracked. It has to be wrecked. [laughter] Oh, you are laughing! You would not stand for a wreck, a moment! A Fool's utterance is total chaos to you because, if you take it, your intellect is deprived of any track upon which to extend its influence in an imaginary unity. Your intellect always involves "you," and that is why your expression is so colored. You allow only that much of "you" to be expressed that is safe from being derailed. *Everyone wants to be berated/B-rated! They do not want to have affixed unto their state a mark of excellence.*

Someone once played very, very well and he was extolled for having played so well. Then the one who was extolled was told that in a way it was a sadness to have achieved this level because now he could never permit himself to drop below that level of excellence.

When you have achieved a letter such as *A* for anything but the Arizona State University, it is a state! When you have accepted the *A* as the Alpha of your life and the *Z* as the end of your alphabet, you had better understand what words are formulated into tonalities that bear a distinction that is not bound by the tonality you hear!

When you choose words that are fitly joined together, you will find that they have, between them, a silence. It is in this silence that so much happens, due to your attention to the beautifully chosen sound-patterns. It is the *soundless* between them that makes each discernible, and yet it is this soundless State unheard (but known to exist by what you hear) that bears the power. This is why it is so important, even in an interview, to perceive the right words that you utilize in expressing what you wish. The right words being heard carry the unheard *Force* that brings change.

Words carelessly put together waste the opportunity offered by someone's attention. That waste is to the one speaking, because that force that allows the words to be heard is immediately consumed by the "Dark Force." This consuming gives the "Dark Force" a semblance of being so intelligent and so clear that it takes a great deal of discernment to perceive how it deceives even the elect.

Words fitly chosen allow a thread of continuity, the silver cord, to be ever bound and yet unfolding.

We think to-day in terms of "a global welfare." We think to-day in terms of bringing harmony and peace and joy and goodwill unto all men. "I come to do Thy Will, O God; the Law is written in my heart." If it is written in the *head*, it bears nothing but a power of taking your attention. It does not bring a change. It brings an emotionalism, and an emotionalism is the evidence of — depth?

You see, *Mind imparts,* and Mind would never impart a lack of confidence. Mind would never impart an inflation of ego. Mind would never impart a lessening of the Great. For *Mind is a string that is strung to the vibrating pulse and heart of Being.* If Mind is on the level of "capital," it should be in the capitals of the world! It really should be the *majuscule*. It should not be registered as *the guiding light;* that has too common a reference to your impressionable needs! Words like that are so accepted because they sound so sweet.

A voice that sounds sweet in correction is a voice that may not have power to correct, and *any voice that is lacking in resonance is a voice that is still "boxed."*

There is nothing stated that should allow you comfort except in your impressionistic state. Remember, you do not create an impression; you *are* an *expression,* because your invisible figure should appear defined. Some have said it is the mark of the five-pointed star and others have said it is a star. I have said:

> **A Star, it broke the sky of time**
> **And it caused a rift. Where?**
> **In the mentality of the mind!**

Why? When it voiced itself, having travelled the light years of ignorance, the language appeared to be the utter- ances of a fool, for it bore no familiarity with the genre of the thought-patterns associated with this little planet. You can- not bring the language of a Star into the broken bits of an asteroid, as so many have tried to do. We have seen so many toying with divine Ideas and they are an *"ass-troyed"*!

If you utilize the words, you must be sure they are in agreement with the clothing of the language that is pertinent unto your inclined, vocal rendition. You cannot allow imper- sonations to keep you on the knee of Edgar Bergen because you are not "Charlies"! You are not "Timothy Totos" but a new beginning! I told you that years ago at university I played successfully the role of Timothy Toto Newbegin, the lunatic in the play, *Outward Bound.* That *was* the part played, and it *is* the part that I play now. It has to be outward bound because it is not *involution* that you are looking after, it is *evolution,* and the movement is from sense to Soul. It is not up or down or sideways, but what have you got? When you cannot go up, you cannot go down, and you cannot go side- ways, what have you got?

Students) Here? Forward?

Well, live by it, whatever you decide. Make your decision and live by it!

What does a face portray? The inner state of the computer! If you have sagging rafters, there is need of support somewhere. Maybe your foundation? How much are you supporting your Foundation?

What do you expect to hear of a global community? What do you expect to experience in the area of a global community? If you are expecting to bring harmony, peace, rhythm, and a melody into cognition of each individual, give it up! You cannot do it. You can lead a horse to water, you can lead an *ass* to water, but you cannot make him drink!

How the mind to-day has shifted in the saddle! The mind to-day tries to saddle a horse that has been well trained in dressage. That horse obeys and knows the slightest movement because the rider is so sensitive and the horse is so sensitive that they are one. There is no point of trying to teach the new rider to be sensitive to the horse if the rider is not in wonder of its throbbing, pulsating body. I am not sure, not having ridden a horse in that form of expertise; I know, though, from the bit I have done, that you have to start to sense the horse beneath you, either you are soon out of the saddle!

As soon as you give people the flowery declarations they want, you can win their votes and their confidence in your dream.

Remember that to-day and to-morrow are made-up of those who can be saddled with the belief of a future and a past. Your force-field bears such an important point. Yours is the point (the point of this moment) that those believers in the past and in the future have multiplied, by thought, into to-morrow and traced into yesterday. *It is the one dot of Presence that is traced. Due to the lack of the ability present to imagine, you cannot see that the dot traced as a line termed "your future" is really one point extended, because you never erased a false identification.*

This is why you have a ruler, because *the ruler knows how you have divided your ability and how much you are utilizing.* A ruler perceives whether you have passed beyond the twelve inches and thus have an entire foot with which to tread, or whether you are still taking baby steps, unsure beyond the crib of the mind.

What is the Master step? It is discipline underfoot. What is the Master's offering? The invisible foot that leaves no imprint in the sand of the Master. In other words, His Presence may be defined by His footprint, but the magnitude will only be known by His ability to release you from the uppers and allow your Soul to come into a vibrating activity.

You all know you are healed, and some say well heeled, and some say, "I wish I could be well-heeled." Of course, if you are ill and wishing for a healing, you all say, "I wish I could be well healed!" If it is because you wish for more money and bring "well-heeled" to a colloquialism, then what you are saying is, *"I wish, but I will not activate it because then I have to be **responsible** for what I **precipitate** by my wish."*

> **You can precipitate anything you wish, if**
> **you are willing to take on the responsibility**
> **of supporting it.**

The reason people appear to be in penury is because they do not want the *responsibility* that comes with being well. *Being well means a healthy expression of involuntary activity.* When your activity is formidable, others may be stunned. But give them the Truth and get rid of the *t* of the stun, and you will find the Sun!

You are like the tree: Your evidence of fruitage allows the one who visited your presence to perceive how all that radiant energy is modulated into a means of accessibility. That has been the action of this One. When you treat this commonly, you allow your thought-garden to be filled with the weeds of laziness, indifference, egotism, and selfishness. It has been said, being too sensitive is really a garment of selfishness. Watch for the over-sensitive people with whom you are dealing, because over-sensitiveness to correction and emotionalism is the evidence of selfishness and a lack of flexibility.

Why is it that you always have an excuse for not having achieved? You have not achieved if you have not been able to support others. If you have not been able to take on other people and support them, for example, by paying for their rent and their food, individually, you have not achieved. There is no point of feeling sorry for yourself; that is the emotion that goes with limit.

The Self does not need to feel sorry for anything. *The Self that I am speaking of does not know anything to feel sorry about; it is only "you" who make "the thing" so important so "you" will not feel left out of the selflessness of Being.*

When you consider this dimension as flat, you do not realize how flat it is until you elevate. Elevate! When you are at seventy-two thousand feet in the air, there is no Earth to be seen because frequently the planet is concealed by clouds. Being so high, your surface is no longer flat; it appears rounded. The one thing you can perceive through the porthole for a moment is the roundness.

It is so black above; you can see the atmospheric levels. You need an atmosphere in your "flat" experience and you create it by creating sets and those who will continue to exploit the same situation of mesmeric flatness of a three-dimensional experience. Three-dimensional experience is not flat, but it always appears that way to one who has moved into a key which takes him out of "wonder" acceptance.

Most people are so timid in coming to face their flat experience that they develop what is termed a neutrality.

This neutrality is confining; it does not allow you to become sharp! If it does, your flat side will not like it. When you realize that you can move a half a step and leave no mark but a tone, your flat side does not like it because your key is present. You *have* to establish keyship! Atonality will not do. That is your world and its chaos. Atonality implies there is no need of keyship; you can use sharps and flats anytime you wish provided you know how to make a natural sign!

A natural sign in formation means that something has changed; in other words, something has been altered. You say, for example (as a neutral and needing to feel not quite so flat), "Mind is in matter." Then if you are sharp, you will say, **"It is Mind instead of matter."** What has happened to your neutrality? You are in the midst of a conflict that arises as a result of a supposition, and it is the original sin! You are born and come to believe that you are "this" and accept it naturally! There are those who have come to say: It is perfectly fine to *appear* to be "this" but know how to make the rugged places plain and the neutral places sparkle in cognition of Reality.

"It doesn't take time to think right" is the most double-edged thought-structure to give to an intellect. It loves it one way and detests it the other way. You know it doesn't take time to *think* (you all agree!), but to say *"right"* means perhaps you may be wrong! There is no "perhaps" about it!

If you are thinking from this plane that is pale in the light of achievement, it is because *you have been prone to a belief system of mediocrity which arises as a result of false identification with the natural state of Being* but perceived by others as a success marking change. If people hear a fine vocal or instrumental performance, they say they are changed. Say, they *are* changed, what marks the difference? They do not bear the expression they did one moment before! Change is always marked by altering the art form, the life form, the action.

When I look upon the sea of faces in the world, it often comes to me: How can I be asked to consider a global community (which I have been asked to consider) and to speak about it, to enliven others about it and to make others excited about it? *Excited* about something! You make somebody excited about something when you know the site and the X becomes the known factor missing to the other individual. The reason something is exciting to me is because I have seen it. You term it "exciting" to you because the X was unknown to you, perhaps, until I cited it for you!

This is what a film-maker does. He perceives what is not perceived and applies it to the stage and, by applying it to the stage, allows the viewer, via the lens of focalization, to lead the attention into the pattern where there is an access to the drama that is yet to be played in order to be perceived.

It is similar in music. The theme is frequently understated. But if it is overstated, it frequently becomes submerged and therefore depends upon the auditor's attention to "fish" it, by the hook of his attention, to the surface for its cognition, as it skims through the conscious clear waters of a pure intention.

Salt water keeps your responses all wrapped up in "you"; fresh water allows the purity of response to come forth in the flowing waters which the streams have. Some lakes are formed from invisible springs from beneath the surface of the ground and some lakes are frequently feeding the rivers; these rivers are all flowing with what is termed "a mild current," and a mild current always washes away the debris and takes it out to sea.

The purity of the Jordan was not in the river; it was what the water stood for under the hand of the One ministering the need for changing the flat surface of experience into the vital dynamics of a prophecy's fulfillment. When I stood by the Jordan and put my hands in the Jordan, it was like the brook in my backyard. What made it holy? A belief that someone very special had stood in this stream; but all those beliefs have been washed away. *What He **was** never stayed in the stream to make it holy; it is what He **was not** that allowed the stream to be termed holy.* To this, the populace gave no regard.

Regard now the state of thy Soul and acquaint thyself with its condition, for it behooves those who have heard the implementing of these Truths that have been set apart from the neutral mind to consider, in this frenetic world where we seem to live and move and have our being, stemming a tidal water and allowing the pure Stream that flows from beneath the throne of God to once again pass over the flat and rugged plains of intellectual attainment and non-attainment, and reveal that if the condition can be described and it is not in keeping with your heart's wishes, it can be changed if you are fortunate enough to know, to hear, to activate, and to don the Conscious-Awareness of a Star.

A Star does not consider from whence it came; it is always seen, for it disturbs the atmosphere of quiescence and yet reveals the leading edge of an unlimited experience, energized, dramatized by the ensuing magnification of expectancy so that the efflux can appear to be found living and man cast beyond the prosaic.

> A guiding Light is such a comfort to those in
> the realm of thought.
> It is such a blessing to have it when you are
> alone and, to it, talk.
> A Light unseen, but known, gives to the
> sincere seeker of peace
> A chance to become acquainted with the
> Silence between the words which one
> speaks.
>
> A guiding Light is present when you see
> within its glow

That the Silence between the presence of
    each word which upon your thought
    does flow
Is no longer a darkness of unknowing but
    the pregnant plane of the bestowal of
    grace,
For 'tis the blessed Silence, the "noise" that
    the mind does not even know and
    forsakes.

Why, the Silence is so powerful, it is like a
    nuclear force.
To your word-like kingdom, it becomes the
    thunder in your "do" course.
The lightning only leaves a mark of
    brilliance where it is found.
It is short-lived and fulfilled when you hear
    the thunder upon the ground.
Remember, to see the lightning and hear the
    thunder, an audience was present to
    sight.
It is how you translated the positive and
    negative by refusing the flat experience
    of life.

Take a neutral position and call it "no-man's
    land."
A guiding Light has promised that if you will
    take the out-stretched Hand,
You can walk the shores of doubt and
    turmoil and find those heights beyond
    the lake or sea
Where you no longer shake in fear of breaking
    under the power of the ensuing years.

The oak was powerful and strong; its roots
    did go so deep.

But it was like the rigidity in mind; there
    was no flexibility in it, so to speak.
But you see, the willow in its simplicity
    allowed a branch to become
Curved and used in a basket. "Son, fetch me
    water, for I thirst!"

Yet, the basket was woven lightly, and the
    Son, who manifested for symbolic sake,
Ran unto the stream ever flowing to satisfy
    what appeared as his Master's thirst,
    for he was awake.
But the Son, he was disquieted, for when the
    basket returned unto the Father of
    Light,
He said, "O my Father of Sunshine, the
    basket is empty, and I have run with all
    my might!"

The Sunshine revealed unto the Son/sun light
    that the basket was only the evidence of
    an act
Of the willingness to do a fantasy, and the
    basket gleamed as That!
The Son said, "O my Father!" and the
    Father said, "Where are you now, my
    Son?"
And the Father's Son laughed, as a Fool
    would laugh when asses try to
    understand such a message of the
    transcendental Sun!

Everyone shall thirst in a land that is flat
    and at ease
With the semblance of exciting news one
    moment and depressing news the
    second — which never does cease.

For the ups and downs, the wavelike
    motion, correspond to an ocean under
    seige
Of a hurricane of doubt and the winds
    blown by selfish deeds.

Will the billows crash upon each other
    before striking the shores of time?
Pray there is a coral reef of protection that
    will allow the shoreline of your mind
To be unruined by a pent-up destruction,
    built upon the refusal to acquiesce to
    the wonder unseen of Might.
The power to the hurricane of suggestion
    was nothing but God trying to impress
    upon you His wondrous might!

The guiding Light did offer a drama.
Where were you when the divine Rama
    struck?
Your shoreline is prepared, for the line that
    has been strung unto you is the One
    Point that didn't come from above, it
    didn't come from beneath,
It didn't come from this side, and it didn't
    come from this side, so why don't you
    seek?

When you find from whence it came, I greet
    you in this heart of Love,
For the omnipotent power of Breath is what
    allows these words to shove
Their way into your dimension where the
    force of space is such
That it takes the mighty power of the Breath
    of the Omnipotent to give these words
    a thrust!

The Breath of the Omnipotent magnified is
    the might unto your gale.
Laugh and enjoy the wonder of how the
    turbulent is made plane.
Don't be pallid and cast down in your
    considerations!
Stand up! and be knocked down by the blast
    that comes with your acquiesence.

In the Light of Love, there is no "me"
    to even trust!
I AM the Love, I AM the Light, and you call
    me a guide, a friend.
You can within your intellectual region, but
    it always has a beginning and end.
For this one so speaking unto you has seen it
    accepted into time,
But it means absolutely nothing to some who
    have taken it and said it was simply
    "divine"!

Promises have been broken; oaths have been
    shattered on the shoals of the mind,
And it is just a wonder-filled blessing that
    my barge still floats on the surge of
    time!
The mast you would try to break by denial;
    you would say there is no wind to fill
    your sails.
You would say, "There is no one on the
    bridge. Where is the captain? There is
    no rudder to prevail!"

I tell you now, the ship was launched in the
    mighty breath of a plea
And it was only "O so help me!" and it
    caused a shimmering sea/C!

To you, it may look like "a glitter"; some
    call it "glamour" unto time,
But those who know the beauty and the
    wonder say, "O it is set apart; it has
    been such a guiding Light!"
Some have called it "a prayer unto the
    divine"!

How do you pray? In silence? Or do you
    talk aloud to find?
And in between each word that is uttered,
    listen! What is it telling?

Thou art divine!

    Thou art divine!

        Thou art divine!

▼

L ook and behold! This world is not a place for just sitting and contemplating; it is a place to create the template of creativity bearing Newness that is forever unique with the attainment.

Chapter XI

The Pleasure of Resistance

robotery

intellect/resistance to change

pain/pleasure

community

energy

Will

Invisible

Unity

The Pleasure of Resistance

We are considering thanks and appreciation for all that is offered in the name of the spontaneous response to unity.

The considerations of to-day are multiple and many, and the concerns are present with everyone. Before launching into an *Unfoldment*™ per se, it came to me that it might be wise to ask if there are any questions that have arisen as a result of study. I am sure you will have many (As a result of no study, there will not be any) because you do not often have a chance to ask me what this Giving means.

You read words, and I wonder sometimes if you ever consider what they mean beyond the page.

> Dina R.) You said recently: "If the world is given back to the arms of Love, it will not be this object that is held in the embrace; it will be freed from being thought an object, as 'you' will be freed from being thought an object and be found not an object just filled with thought but an object to testify that there is more than thought!" Sir, "giving the world back to the arms of Love" has been an

> intriguing phrase that you have often used. How do we see the world in the realm of ideation?

That is the only way you see it, through the realm of ideation and imagination. It comes with the experience of breathing in and breathing out and the acceptance of birth. It has always remained what it is. Without the breath, the body is said not to be; therefore, there is no mind, no space for an object to appear in it and, therefore, no time. It only exists in your realm of projection; it does not exist at all in the *unity that IS.* You are never without it, but you are never within it. It does not mean it *is not* and it does not mean it *is;* it just means that it is not what you *think* it is, and what it is, it is not! But you are never worried about it, because *no matter where you are, you will always have what is essential to satisfy the fullness of your creativeness.*

> Dina R.) Is that what is meant by "I will not leave you comfortless"?

That is what is meant to one who is in the throes of approaching initiation. "I will not leave you comfortless" points to death; and, of course, the embryo thinks it is dying when it leaves the womb, but we call it *birth.* The embryo usually comes head first, but we seem to walk on our feet. Would it not be surprising if we were really walking on our heads, and we could not stand the suggestion, so the mind turns our feet onto the bottom and puts our head on the top?! The picture is all upside-down, anyway; it is only in the last rites of the eyes' operation that it is transformed by the brain to an upright position!

Yes, Barry.

> Dr. Barry B.) Mr. Mills, I refer to a passage in your book, *Tyranny of Love,* in the chapter, "The Quickening Spirit of Radiance, Part

Two." There is a phrase that I have heard you use for twenty years and I thought I knew what it meant: "knowing what you know." I used to think that I knew what I knew. The statement that is in the *Unfoldment*™ is: "You will never know *what* you know until you decide to be Real!"[1] I don't know if mine is a question but rather a resonance with that statement. The activation of the knowing for me, of late, has not been an intellectual one, because when I have not had the scaffolding of the mind, or not been able to rely on the mind in any way, that knowingness is something that is so deep —

It is.

Dr. Barry B.) — that I could not get away from it if I tried.

That has been the result of your pain; that is why you have had the pain. It has been a blessing in disguise, because you are too precious to have been allowed to think that your intellect, in its cleverness, would yield the fruits of achievement. So you now know that it is not the intellect that yields the fruits of achievement; those are the fruits of the garden that the intellect yields. That is why *knowing* is such a treasurable thing, because *knowing is that state that is precipitated as one ceases to be compressed by a false sense of identity, which rests primarily with the intellect. When you come to distrust your intellect, all you have left is the knowing that you Are, even without the declaration. That is the knowing that is the key to opening the door to the fullness of the unified State.*

You are approaching that; in fact, you have approached it; in fact, you are "in" it. Everyone in this room is "in" it, but

---

1. Kenneth George Mills, *Tyranny of Love* (Stamford and Toronto: Sun-Scape Publications, 1995), p. 41.

due to the thinking process and the false-identity process and the cleverness of the intellectual assumptions, we find ourselves "excluded" from that incredible State.

> Dr. Barry B.) I know that what you say is true, Mr. Mills. You have given so many hints and clues and practices to help us to distrust the mind. I tell you, if we used just *one* of them, it would be incredible.

This said with sincerity is a keynote to freedom. Yes, Gwynne.

> Gwynne M.) Sir, you have said that the "parent-child" is the seed of community.

Yes, it is.

> Gwynne M.) You asked us to consider it, and I have considered it at some length but would love you to explicate it. It seems that there are so many levels on which it could be understood.

What have you considered?

> Gwynne M.) On the highest level, the acknowledgment of the Father, that I am the Son, and that that is a unified state. There is no separation. I have considered the parent-child from the standpoint of the child or from the standpoint of the parent as one of responsibility.

No. The standpoint of the child and of the parent is the standpoint of suggestion. A community is a very important subject, and the parent-child or the child-parent relationship is terribly important. It is the seed idea and it is brought into just two words, *parent-child, child-parent,* as a seed in a husk. When it is planted in the correct soil and nurtured, it develops roots and blossoms.

What are some of the basic stumbling blocks to community?

> Nora B.) Mr. Mills, could there be a resistance to dominance or correction?

You have used one of the most important words: *resistance.*

Yes, Mary-Joy.

> Mary-Joy L.) Would it not also be resistance to change?

Those are very important words, and you are going to see why in a minute.

Why do you find that people who go into communities spend so much time complaining? Why do you find that people always find something wrong with someone in the house, and if they do not, they bury it under a lot of rubbish and pretend everything is fine when it is not?

Perhaps one of the reasons that people do not want community is because they do not wish to *affirm another's meaning;* they do not wish to allow *another's expression,* if the one dares to express. No one wants to give up the feelings aroused by confrontations on the subtlest level, arguing and fighting over nothing, because this gives the one a feeling of separateness and of importance.

There is a resistance, as Nora said, and people love resistance; it is pleasure. That is how interesting our intellect has become. *Our greatest pleasure is resistance* because resistance always implies separateness: "I am myself, I have my own space, and that is that! I have my own way of thinking; I don't think as you think." That is one who will never be in a community, because in a community you cannot have that attitude present, because resistance creates an army of likeness.

The whole force-field of Light rests on unity. This means that resistance, which arises as a result of person, is subdued with the arisal of the cognition of correct Identity. Therefore, the incorrect communication, the resistance, and the lack of constant endeavor imply a constant enhancement of "me, me, me, me, me."

Every time you do not fulfill something you say you will do, it is the most incredible satisfaction to "you"; it creates a sense of "importance" that you do not have, other than through your resistance to fulfillment! Anyone who fulfills a job is seldom cognized for it. I live to bear witness to that! It is when you resist and make a fuss that your whole sense of importance is underlined in the realm of delusion.

The community will never be founded if you cannot affirm and accept another's presence as one in the act of rescinding a false identity. Everyone entering a household should be entering it to rescind the response that comes from *selfishness*. That selfishness arises when you feel that you do not want to do something at that moment when you have said you would do it, and you decide to be miserable about it and try to make everyone else miserable! Believe it or not, people succeed.

If you are miserable in your thought, you are contaminating the entire atmosphere of the world and supporting the entire atmosphere of delusion and destruction and decay. *Robotery is such a force-field of fear, and people are enhancing it more and more because a fearful people are filled with separateness, and this is why it is such a pleasure. It is a false sense of pleasure, but it is so pleasurable that you will not give up your separateness.* (This is how you might consider it.)

If you bear horrid thoughts but you have a smiling face, then —

> "There was a little girl
> Who had a little curl
> Right in the middle of her forehead;
> And when she was good
> She was very, very good,
> But when she was bad, she was horrid!"[2]

It is very true, unfortunately. If you go on *bearing* these thoughts, *burying* these thoughts, you are actually fortifying error and disease. This is why there is the inclination to remain more and more apart from everything. I know the important charge I carry and I know it is not going to be minimized by the faulty thought-atmosphere surrounding my thought-appearance, because I AM more than an appearance projected by your attention into your dimension of experience.

There is no more time or leniency with false patterns of attention to the lecture called *Unfoldment*™ and to its effect, called Realignment. A realignment to what?

Students) Principle.

Yes. To Principle. And what is Principle, to you?

Student) The Source, Sir?

Yes. And what is the Source? *The Source is everything "you" are not! But due to it, you seem to be!* That is the graciousness of it. That is the graciousness of the Light: It allows one to appear to be just like you and yet not the least bit like any of you. But it is "the hell" of the appearance, too, because this means that one has to enact roles that are totally part of the scenario of your belief system.

---

2. Henry W. Longfellow, "There Was a Little Girl."

What is a belief system?
The basis of the seeding of robotery.

Yes, Nurit.

> Nurit O.) Thank you, Sir. Last night I was at
> the offices, looking at your paintings, and it
> just amazed me to see the evidence of your
> accomplishment. There are so many things
> that you did in such a short time, there is the
> music, the painting, there is the new CD, there
> is all the work that you have done with the
> EarthStage Actors, and the new book; all the
> books were there, and it goes on and on.
> There is so much, and it was such a humbling
> experience; it was almost embarrassing to feel,
> How could a man do so much when we have
> done so little? After considering that this is the
> result of the actions being totally free and
> being so pure, the words "I **will** to do Thy
> Law" were heard in such a different way.

Will is basically volition. Volition cannot exist without
energy. *What is energy the evidence of? Enlightenment?*
Energy is the mark of Mastership. Energy is a mark of
emancipation; a lack of energy marks the levels that are
needed to attain. Energy, directed and perceived, is the
Source of your experience; *personalized,* it is deterioration
and limit. If energy is evidenced in cognition and recognized
as the very Source of activity, as all there is, then attainment
is sure.

Most people are so devoid of energy. It is the level
of the neophyte. The first mark of the first degree of attainment is the evidence of an enhancement in *constant energy.*
People wonder where they are in the attainment? All they
have to do is see how constant energy is and then see how
constantly they fluctuate due to the pleasure of resistance.

What is the greatest pleasure of resistance? Being able to lecture to somebody else, being able to tell somebody else what things mean! One of the greatest forms is standing-up intellectually and telling other people off because they "do not know." Without having to talk to me, it reveals to you where you are at!

All you have to do is look at the emasculated men and the women and consider: *What is one doing that is allowing or not allowing one's associates to come to the fullness of their experience?* Are you considering your expression as one that will stop the errant thoughts and allow one to realize his or her wonder? Or are you just hearing yourself talk to enjoy pleasure while another feels the pain of being made "smaller"? Another form of pleasure! Some will say, "It is so painful to be made to feel I have attained nothing." If you are thinking that or feeling that, it shows you why you have not appeared to have much energy.

You always have energy to do what you want to do. You always have energy to keep back what you want to keep back. You always have energy to get attention by being late for your jobs, by not fulfilling your jobs on time, by having to go back and finish them, by not doing a good job the first time. *This is the limitation of the race: it lives now on a fractured limb of engagement.*

We were all supposed to be custodians of special gifts. There is not one person in this room and there is not one person hearing my voice, and there is not one person responding to this vibratory frequency — not one is untouched or unaffected, because from that Point from which this force is issuing, there is no largeness of a symbol even to be considered. This force-field is reaching and penetrating and enhancing every other energy that is in keeping with this force, wherever it is.

The mind that cannot conceive that you are not "this" will never conceive that I AM That! There is no possible way to explain it even though it is "a rough plane and the rugged places shall be made plain"! That one is pretty rugged! It cannot be made plain because your mind is too jagged and it is too impertinent. It tries to minimize the declarations of non-resistance. It tries to minimize that pleasure and pain are any different.

Most people are so concerned about pain, they do not know how to use it. It is said that the teachers of the past inflicted it upon their students because pain was one way of causing one to transcend the sensorial and move into a level of what is termed "death." That is how Paul could say, in Corinthians, "I die daily," because *to die daily meant that you suffered the pain of this formation and knew you were not it.* Every time you feel pained, use it to realize that if you feel it, then that part of you that is perceiving the pain is not in it, and the part of you that is perceiving pleasure is not in it. *Pleasure and pain are the divisions of the sensorial: each may be pleasurable, each may be painful, but in truth they are not.* If they were, pain would be an eternal attribute of God, pleasure would be an eternal attribute of God; pain would be an attribute or a synonym of Principle, and pleasure would be a synonym of Principle, but *pain and pleasure are the seeming conditions of the formation.*

Communities are so lacking in the world because in a situation where there is a lack of attainment, there is such a reluctance *to affirm another.*

What is a group extension? It is the inclusiveness of the knowing that the separateness is for the play, each has his part and each one is fulfilling it according to his intention. **The Work of Realignment** is allowing, through the acceptance of an Ideal such as God, Source, Energy, Principle, any of the Synonyms of God to be the Ideal around which all your thought-structures dance in order for the maypole to be more than just a seasonal experience! If that pole is the staff or *the rod of clear intention or Principle defined in your life action,* then you *may* do this and you *may* do that.

It is not a matter of "can" or "can't." "May" does not involve "can" or "can't." In other words, you may be positive and you may be negative; it all depends on what you consider your pole to be: the rod of right Identification or the transitory experience of a temporary allegiance to a passing fancy.

When you are pressed, why do you feel it? When you press your skirts or when you press your dresses or your trousers after taking them off — what happens when you press? You get out all the wrinkles under the steam and the heat! You do not expect a wrinkle to remain. When you are pressed, why do you feel that it is so noteworthy to scream as each wrinkle disappears? "I am so changed. Don't you notice a change in me? Look, I am wearing my lipstick on my teeth! Don't you see such a change in me? My hair is falling out." You know? "Why don't you see such a change in me?" *That change is not marked necessarily by just the appearance; it is marked by the altering effect of your presence, or of Presence.* (I say "your" just so I will not totally wipe you out!) By *your* Presence. The altering effect of "your" Presence is that others feel an accent that they had not felt until they met you. If people work with you daily and they do not feel this, then your presence is compressed into the formation of a personality and its complexes. But press on!

What is the point? If you were really going beneath the surface, you would be vocalizing an entirely different verbal melody and your speech would be like song. I wonder how many have studied two or three hours a day? There is no doubt that out of twelve hours you have all spent most of ten in the realm of the unreal. It is something to be quiet within yourself and yet have all kinds of noise around you!

That is the way I lived my life until I escaped from it, because I realized, after all, there was an Exemplar called Jesus and there was no better example anywhere. He went to the mountaintop to get away from everyone. He screamed and He sobbed and wept because no one was getting the message. They were not even impressed with the fact that there was not one thing in the prophetic books that He was not fulfilling. They did not want to accept the prophetic books because if they did and He was the fulfillment of them, it meant that all things had to be made new. They would have to cease considering themselves compressed into a race or into a nation or into the origin of each, a unit of "child and parents" or "parents and child." That is why I said "parent-child" without the s, because "child and parents" or "parents' child" is signifying you and your efforts, but "parent-child" or "child-parent" is quite a different vibratory frequency. We are dealing with the embryo as the parent-child.

What is the point of a child if the parent still believes he did it or she did it? The whole idea that fosters the sense of production is the need to feel separate but indirectly connected. It is so fascinating. It is said that as soon as the mother has the child, the husband takes second place. I know that this is the general consensus: the father takes second place. The child becomes the more important; it becomes the focus of attention because frequently it is the mother who says, "Look! I have birthed this beautiful child." She did, but it is a miracle, it is a wonder. If she personalizes, you know it because when you are not nice to her, she says, "Look at the pain you've caused me. Look at what I've given you all my life. Look at what I've spent on you, and you treat me this way." Immediately the personalization from the very beginning of that relationship points to the exact turmoil in your community, in your village, in your nation, and in the world.

The aboriginals felt that after being birthed children should stay with the mother, who could feed them and nurse them, look after them for a couple of years; then they would be given over to the tribe. Then they would be taught by the elders, by the wise men. They did not even know it, or perhaps they did, but by minimizing the association of parents and the child, they moved out of a scenario of limitation and mesmerism. A metaphysician once said that

anyone wishing a child should consider well the purpose for
wishing a child. Question deeply within yourself why you
would wish a child, because, after all, you may be wishing
upon him a perpetuation of a lie and a dream. Shocking!?

What is the essential point of all high Teaching?
Shocks! Gurdjieff said that you could never move into
another octave without a shock. **The only shock people can
get to-day is from having their patterns of identity put to
question. When those patterns are put to question, the
answer starts to loom on another weaving entirely; it weaves
another pattern entirely.**

> It weaves a pattern of energy that is usually
> garmented in *Love* if it is to transform,
> garmented in *Truth* if it is to shock,
> garmented in *Spirit* if it is to prevail,
> garmented in *Soul* if it is to be felt,
> garmented in *Principle* in order to stabilize,
> garmented in *Mind* in order to give
>   confidence to the errant one,
> and garmented in the realization that the
> *Source,* the *Energy, God,* is what allows even the
> misunderstood to be and yet not to be.

It is a time when community is not just a little thought
for a small group of people. Perhaps the reason community is
coming to your thought is because you people know enough
intellectually to subdue a belief-pattern surrounding identity to a knowing experience. When you consider the various
examples of the Teaching that you have had, and I have had
as a result of offering these lectures over these twenty-seven
years, if I did not know what is known, I would not be here,
because *there is no evidence that what I have given has been
assumed as a vital aspect of life.*

It is fascinating, the problems that are confronting people to-day are the same problems that were confronting
Socrates, confronting Pythagoras. He gave a key: that there

was meaning to every symbol, and no number should ever confuse or deny the existence of the Invisible, for even *one* arose from it. It was part of the sacred teachings of Egypt, to give your false identity an opportunity to be able to perceive intellectually the transient nature of itself and the changeability of itself.

It was pointed out that the beginning of numerology was the invisible, called zero, out of which came *one*. Who conceived *two*? Two could only be conceived as one recognizing one. That is how there is the possibility of being fitly joined: One recognizing One; in other words, One affirming another's correctness. This is the only possible way that anything new could appear. Out of the recognition of affirming another's presence as viable, recognition dawned. From that point on, numbers became unlimited. You can see what a difficulty two is, because two points intellectually to more than one, but to *knowing* ("It takes One to know One") it is reduced to unity!

One of the prime purposes of an Unfoldment™ *is not to clarify the intellect but to put it into question as capable of understanding that which used it and was not it.* It is great, but it is also imperative that you start to perceive how the thoughts you hold are either helping or damming the wealth, the welfare, the well-being, the commerce, the finance, life in general. Your fluctuation is evidenced in the stock market. Look where you bet and what you gamble upon! You bet and gamble on your prowess at argument: "I have a right to think this way," "I have a right to my own space," "I want to live alone so that I can feel my separateness." That is why there is no community, because each wants to be separate and have his own way. The old hymn says, "Have Thine own way, Lord. Have Thine own way." *The Lord is the fulfilling of the Law, and if it says that all shall be returned unto the Father, it means that all shall be reduced to One. Why One? Because one is the symbol of unity, and the zero which supports it says it is infinite, which means it is beyond anything that the mind can comprehend.*

Utilize every consideration that comes to you and see whether or not it is enforcing your position in gaining attention. Now, mind you(!), there has to be a board of directors, there have to be stenographers, there have to be servants, there have to be people willing to do everything I have done and everything I am doing. *That is the way it appears to you, but I have only done all these things to resist the confinement of personality.*

Someone who was told of my art said, "Oh, it's just another one of Mr. Mills' hobbies." He saw it to-day for the first time (he is quite learned in this field) and was very discombobulated upon seeing it; he would not admit it because of his personality and his resistance to what confronted him as Himself. He settled, and within two hours it was a total revelation. He said what he liked and what he did not like and what he liked in this painting and what he did not like, but at the end of the meeting he said, "These are remarkable! Every one I am looking at on these walls is remarkable." It was fascinating because that was not the statement when he first saw them. He said, "You know, I didn't see that when I first looked. Oh, I didn't see *that* when I first looked. This is amazing!" The paintings were there all along, but *what he was perceiving was the obvious change in his resistance.*

> Resistance precludes perception.
> Compression precludes expression.

Community comes to your attention because it is a worldwide consideration. A moment ago, I mentioned robotery. All your computers are so seductive because they allow you to communicate without feeling. They are very seductive. They are very mesmeric because by communicating without feeling, you have an enhanced sense of separateness, and yet capability. This is how it is birthed. You will find that computers are a great benefit in one way, and yet they are worse than the television tube because they are being utilized to do what you were supposed to be able to do without them.

Remember, the computer is the result of a mind revealing its ability to program in a way that others in agreement with it would accept. A programming on computers is like a religion; it has followers. It becomes so common that you do not realize the mesmeric nature of it. You can be very creative on it, but no one has to see the creation of your monstrosities; they can be erased. That is why, in painting, I do not like to work *over* a painting; each stroke should be direct. When my sister first saw me paint, she said, "I am amazed at how direct you are with every stroke." It is that directness that is not considered. *You are never as direct if you consider, but you have to be directed before you consider without directness!*

You cannot be personally feeling a superior position and direct successfully. You seem to be in a superior position because you know *there is only One Director as a result of the infinite.* Then you can appear to direct.

Cognition does not necessarily mean presence; it frequently means withdrawal if there is a poor self-image. *Withdrawal is always a lack of self-esteem.* You cannot wear jewelry, you cannot wear beautiful clothes with ease and suitableness if you are concerned. You cannot if you are ill-at-ease with being as you really are, because the vibratory frequency that supports this appearance also supports gold. **Gold is nothing but the condensation of wonder.** That is why men were crowned with it.

The reason the great diamond is worn in the crown is because it was *the crown jewel of discrimination.* Why? When discrimination was found capable of being utilized within seven breaths, each breath was a string of attunement to the Synonyms of Reality, or to the strings of the heart, or to the rhythmic beat of creation! That is why the fetus upon birthing into form (or the seed birthing into form) is immediately placed to the heart, so that what was within the heart, floating within the blissful sea of effortlessness, is now put into another dimension *but the one continuing factor is the rhythm of Being.*

Robotery causes you to forget the rhythm of your heart. It causes you to forget wonder. It causes you to be wrapped up in personal resistance. Every problem that comes up on the computer is a resistance. People make such a problem out of an opportunity. A problem exists for those lacking in self-esteem. They make problems out of their lives! That is the problem of which I am speaking. They make problems out of their lives *instead of using life as an opportunity to express creativeness.* Why to express *creativeness?* Because the essence of energy is its unlost ability always to Be! That is why it is said, "Energy is never lost."

▼

Chapter XII

Inherent Fire

mind/thinking

self-esteem

imagination

wonder

Identity

Energy/Force

Inherent Fire

Have you ever stopped to consider how it is that everyone seems to experience the same world? If you have, then tell me how. Yes, Neal.

Neal D.) We give consent to the same images; we are agreeing —

Yes. That is getting close to what is meant by that question. It is due to each one bearing the conduit of an essential idea, and the same essential idea that matches formation, which has all been achieved as a result of a faculty of imagination. If imagination is at the root of your world, what is your imagination?

Jennifer M.) Is it energy, Sir?

Yes, it is energy — the Source, energy. But what is *imagination?* Imagination is a faculty that everyone possesses. It goes with the idea of your world and your form. It is the source of image-making. Have you ever considered that *the source of your image-making is energy, when most of you appear devoid of it?* If you are all the result of image-making, how come you are so quick with the intellectual answer of "energy" and "Source"? You tell me now that you are the result of image-making, yet you are devoid of energy and vitality! Is energy static?

Students) No, Sir.

Then, will you tell me, what are "porcelain-ized" faces if they are not appearing as the disease as manifested on the robot? It is amazing how deeply people have considered that energy is the source of their image-making, which results in the experience of imagination of your world and the people that dwell therein. But if the Source is energy, why do people appear so devoid of it? Is *energy ever lost?* No! If it is never lost, then it must always have evidence! If you are sitting still, the only evidence of its presence is the constant changing of your responsive nature, appearing on your faces. That is why, when you perceive an audience sitting with rapt attention and porcelainized faces, you know that they are *thinking*. They are not responding to the invisible feathers of Light which cause them to smile.

If you are the custodians of such an incredible faculty, then you perceive without doubt the wisdom that gave unto Nathanael, one of Jesus' disciples, the power termed "imagination." The only place to give it was to the feet of an accepted Messianic figure because it had to be redeemed. The redemption of a faculty is termed "liberation," and in the Christian terminology, it is termed "*Christ*ened." To believe and to be taught that there is but one Christ is the very root of bondage. It does state that "He who hath seen Me hath seen the Father." It does not say, other than through your speculation, that there was only Jesus. Jesus is part of your imagination, as I am, and you are a part of each other's imagination.

The demand of the Age is to be precipitated by the awareness program of Light into the restored Upper Room of attainment. When we go to the Upper Room, we are said to pray for what is needed and we are supposed to go up to attain it; in other words, we are supposed to utilize intellectual thoughts about a mediator. But it was the very enlightened state of the great Exemplar that said a mediator state was disastrous; that was only for the neophyte. He said, "I and my Father are One," and all those who heard it screamed and shouted and tooted, "Blasphemous!" just as many in the church would to-day. But if those who are attending churches do not perceive they are ordained — that is the reason they are in the audience. The schooled and intellectually trained mediators are supposing that the simplicity of Being guileless and pristine in nature is not worthy of conception *unconfined.*

There is no limitation other than what you think. There is no fear other than in the lack of yearning; there is no fear other than in the refusal to hear. There is no *fear*[1] other than in not earning the right to a constant volition.

The entire "printed realm" is *thought* into importance. Why? Because it is said it is *heard* to exist. **The printed realm is *thought* into existence because it is *heard* to exist.** That is why you are in such a pleasant position, because without *knowing,* you are being spoken to *as if you do.* In print this lecture will not have the same meaning, because the printed word does not offer hearing, and your faculty is then diminished in translation.

How can you translate a symbol into force if you do not know the condition of the symbol appearing as yourself, a moving symbol?! *How can you translate a printed symbol into meaning when you have not even looked at what is causing you to live and to move and have your being, and frequently erupting,* "I can think this if I want to. I don't care"?

The mind exists in your imagination. Your imagination has endowed it with thinking ability, considering ability,

---

1. Mr. Mills has referred to the word "fear" in a redeemed sense as the "Father's ear." See other words in this context above, all containing "ear": *earn,* heard, hear.

thought ability. Why does it not function in the name of original talent? I strip the imagination to its essential feature. *The essential feature of the mind present is thinking. What does the mind evidence? Thought.* What is the mind made-up of?

Students) Thoughts.

Can you change your mind?

Students) Yes.

Then it is not the one to depend on! *That is why the redeemed imagination leads you to the Mind that is unchangeable.* The Mind that is unchangeable is perceived; it is not hidden. It only has to be revealed, and the Mind that IS is revealed by Truth. *What is Truth? Thought. But what is the result? Force. That is why it is Truth, like Love, that sets the captive free. Why? Because the Truth-thought can be known as an effect!* Thinking Truth allows the thoughts to conform to what is true. *And what is true? The acceptance of the constant Source: energy.* If you have "a thought" that you feel depleted, dissatisfied, challenged, your mind is regurgitating the thoughts of the unenlightened or the robotic nature. Intellect given to the scenario of repetition of standardized, theoretical, scientific explanations and explorations gives you a world in conflict.

The world is said to be given back to the arms of Love. Why do we use "the arms of Love"? Because it is an embrace. The only way you can embrace the world is as it is: a common image bestowed upon everyone who takes this form of objectivity. Therefore, *the only way the world can be given back to the arms of Love is to be embraced as a divine Idea,* because it seems to persist in constancy. That is the mark between a divine or infinite Idea and a finite one. An infinite is constant, as the seven Synonyms are constants.[2] *Everything else is finite, transitory, and unstable.*

---

2. Mary Baker Eddy, *Science and Health with Key to the Scriptures* (Boston: Trustees Under the Will of Mary Baker G. Eddy, 1934), p. 465, ll. 8-15.

Your whole state is so questionable, either you would not be delving so much into the realm of entertainment. Entertainment is the escape route of robotery, unless the entertainment is approached from the standpoint of knowing. To go to a concert when you know the analytical persuasions of a composition, and to go to a concert when you know them not, makes the experience entirely different. The one who knows the musical analysis and construction and architecture of a composition hears quite a different performance from one who takes a tonal bath. One who knows *this* performance is having a very different experience from one who is just sitting here not having studied and done an analytical, depth search. Those who have not done this will not hear this other than as a tonal bath. This is why it says: **Study to find yourself approved. Approved for what? For leaving your mind!**

The self-righteousness and the egotism in the world! *Do you realize?!* I would hope so, but few do. *What is the great weakness en masse of to-day's world?* (There are so many weaknesses, I am wondering if you have ever considered this one in particular.) *It is the lack from which everyone suffers, that of wrong identification.* Everyone has such a shallow sense of *self-esteem.* Your self-esteem is so "essential" that you have to depend upon your birth to get it from those who are close to you. It is such a phony concept; it has to do with the pseudo-way of the robot.

Thanksgiving for what? For perceiving the need of correct Identity! Then, basically, correct Identity cannot have anything to do with personality, because your problem is your personality! People have got so much of it; it is the disease of the age.

How many of you express Identity? What is Identity? The mark that is not left by an i-dot! *The mark of Identity is the Presence that causes change involuntarily.* What causes change involuntarily? To know the Truth that sets you free: *that the source of your freedom is in a redeemed imagination*. In other words, your energy bears a common seed, and that common seed is not only the world and people like you; it is Conscious-Awareness of your form that exists!

You cannot separate Energy from having a corresponding identity. It is not "your" movement; it is Conscious-Awareness that perceives the movement. You *think* movement; you *know* awareness! You *think* activity; you *source* awareness. Why do you go to the library to source for knowledge (and you obviously find most of it vain)? Why is it vain? It enhances self-esteem. This is why, unless perceived correctly, scholarship inflates. Look at the graduates of universities! Did you ever see more self-evident superiority dressed-up in blue jeans and beards? Speak to it; it is so rare that you find any one of them capable of dropping at the feet of wonder! If they drop at the feet of *wonder,* they suddenly *realize*. It is like the Polish people: *wonder* is not a word used in their vocabulary to-day. How much is it used in your vocabulary with *knowingness* instead of *thoughtfulness?*

If Man is more than person and has really no limit of a personality, is this not a cause for your withdrawal symptoms from the drug abuse of your mind? Why would you not love it? It allows you to enter a whole new Identity as you *really are*. As you succumb to the wonder of Conscious-Being, embracing this figment of the imagination, with its gentility and forcefulness at the same time, it should give you the apprehension of what it means to be God-bearing-force. **You may appreciate** *this;* **it behooves you to know** *That!* You should not try to understand by your intellect what has been said; it should be fitted to your needs and worn as *a garment to experience.*

Why is it said that the Great have always had disciples and their greatness was always evidenced (supposedly) by the disciples? Because *in the aura of the Great, man can find the verification or the authenticity of his movement. The force-field is such that if one is off-pitch, one hears the dissonance in the encounter. The only cadence that can be written is for the dissonance to resolve.* It is back of all composition. *People have forgotten that dissonance has only one point: to move.* Maybe this is one reason that great music is rarely being written, because there are no great states of Conscious-Awareness to *boo* the pseudo-achievement.

A great composition cannot come from a composer who is not penetrating the mystery of existence. It is one thing to be talented musically, but talent is like a diamond in the rough: It looks like a piece of coal until it is cut and polished and put through the wheels that grind exceedingly small but go as fast as hell!

I had the opportunity, in Holland, to visit with a professor of diamond cutting; I spent the morning with him as he was teaching his students. It was fascinating. Some of you were with me when we viewed the huge black diamond; it would have been nice to have put it on your wrist as an ornament! Although it was beyond price, a black diamond was worthless as an object to look at; it looked like a piece of onyx. No matter how they cut it, it did *not* reveal a fire!

What made the black and the white diamond different? *The black had the fire but could not manifest it; cut by a master, the white diamond revealed the innate fire which made it precious.* You are like that! Why do you go on being like a piece of polished anthracite or bituminous coal, hard or soft? The diamond is the hardest known precious stone. Next to it are the sapphire and the emerald. But the emerald is brittle, it can break like a piece of glass. This is why it has to be worn with such care. You have to be very aware of your hand and your finger when you are wearing the emerald because it is very fragile.

The value of the emerald, of course, is the depth of its color. Today there is seldom one found that does not have an inclusion. It is so fascinating, the inclusion proves that it is real, just like the star sapphire or the star ruby. *When it is synthetic, the star is static, like words; the star cannot move. It is only in the authentic that the star reveals itself according to the light of perception.*

When I wear it, if you can sit where you can see the star sapphire, *you can see the star move to where you are with all its five brilliant points. If the light is diffused by a cloud of suggestion, the star does not allow itself to be seen, because you are not in the condition to perceive its reality!* I went into a jewelry store once, a very prominent one in New York. I do not think they expected to see this sapphire. They looked at it and said, "Is that synthetic?" and I said, "Look!"

The preciousness of any condition is evidenced by its inherent fire. It is only when the diamond is fully cut with fifty-eight facets that the full fire can be revealed, provided there is not an inclusion that refracts the light within it. If it is in the main body of the diamond, there is a perception of a flaw and the diamond is not so valuable. The diamond may have a flaw on the rim of it, but if it is in the body, it alters the value.

It takes the magnification power (in other words, the view of your ordinary sight would not reveal it), and when the sight is magnified, you can look *through* the suggested object and perceive the uniqueness that marks a natural state. It has nothing whatsoever to do with a cultivated, intellectual, ascertained evaluation of the stone.

It does not give you self-esteem to wear a diamond; it does not give *me* this pleasure at all. It simply represents *the Fire that I know is the Source of the dynamics of life.* It does not matter if it is large or small, provided you place a value on what you wear on your finger. Each one is a digit of wonder, for each can point to a key of significance, or can be used to execute the demise of a limit. You cannot finger your way through the leaves of historical data with the intellectual prowess of years of restricted learning and expect to see the wonder before the page! *If you do not have wonder, your library is left unread;* it takes too much time and energy, when you could be entertained by a football or a hockey game .. or by a concert! *Why do you not sponsor the arts by knowing the wonder of a creative genius? Experience it as your Self! Art is what another calls the simplicity of your Real intention!*

Do not resist being Real! It is the only way "you" can get attention, but I would be *dammed* from the flow of my life if I believed "your" experience as Real.

Do you feel yourselves dammed by viewing my experience with the biases and the jealousies and the enviousness with which you may view me? If you cannot perceive the beauty and the grandeur and the magnitude of simplicity manifesting, then you will never experience it yourself! If you are in need, consider how your thoughts are inhibiting the conduit of eternal Light! The way you make contact is by expecting to hear and declaring, "I heard!" It said, "Come unto Me if you pray, and suffer the pains of birth!"

Being new is not an intellectual pleasure, it is hell! You confront every thought-pattern that you think identifies your personality with its god-damming charm. When you have not got it you create a "pleasant" personality? It is like attending to the flowers that you put on a grave. A pleasant personality is a living tombstone of what might have been! Most people have it engraved on the faces of their stone: *"Here lies the intellectually bound to the attrition of supposition and the refusal to exculpate voluntarily from this self-incarceration, just to remain comfortable in the same orbit of mediocrity!"* If that is your choice, *stay there!* It is entirely up to you. "Whom shall ye choose: God or mammon?" God is the Truth, and mammon is what you dream-up to be the Truth when it is not! *Truth is a constant, and mammon is changeable.*

The Elohim is extensive, extending, and embracing; not going up to heaven or down to hell, or east to west as the zephyr does blow. It is the force that radiates from the Fire of the Center that man cannot know intellectually; but when that Fire is known by surrender to it, the words appear to be heard by the "no-thinker" as well as by the thinker who wishes to know!

Thank you. See you to-night, and we will continue to crush the leaves of the Sage! *What is the point of sage? It lives to be crushed, in order for its fragrance to remind you of its kinship with the aroma of Being!*

▼

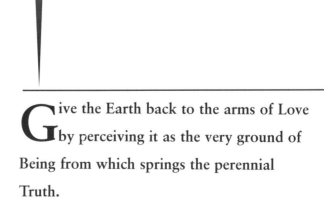

G ive the Earth back to the arms of Love
by perceiving it as the very ground of
Being from which springs the perennial
Truth.

Chapter XIII

A Verbologist's Wonder

intellect/computers

acceptance/understanding

visible

yearning

rebirth

Verbology/language

stride in two worlds

Love's freedom

Soul/Invisible

A Verbologist's Wonder

This is a continuing act in the profession of my calling. I am a verbologist attempting to deal with "herbologists"! You have to do so many things to herbs in order to have them ready for consumption.

Tell me, what right do you have? What if I tell you, you have a very important right? **"You have a right *not* to be negative."** Try it. It is hell! Test it. It is hell!

We are continuing the discovery of that initiatic experience which has been termed *Unfoldment,*™ which is now known to be considered applicable to the side of life, of appearance, as **Realignment,** in order to stem the tide of suggestion and reduce it to the pulp of the unused psychic force-field of mind.

You are endowed with many gifts, for if you have perceived, you know That for which you yearn is now a possibility of receiving. *Are you ready to accept it?* It is one thing to say commendable remarks when asked *"What are you yearning for?"* but a salient feature of all the answers is this: They are all pointing to an exemplary condition and wish, but you have leapt over a requirement due to the intellectual agility of your thieving intellect. It has not told you, you cannot achieve your yearning without achieving *freedom. Freedom from what? The false conditions of personality! You have to be freed from personality dressed-up as if it were holy because it has the jargon of a spiritual basis.*

A jargon of a spiritual basis is utilized for those who are wishing to worship something tentatively. The jargon of empowerment causes an eruption within the mental configurations, for *when you start to think of freedom, you start to be confronted with your intellectual chaos which has you falling madly in love with and devoted to your masquerade and its party.* You dress-up for a masquerade, but it was never meant for you to forget that it is inevitable that it must fall.

What is the inevitable that must fall? The intellectual configurations that cannot withstand the blast of Light! This is why those who are not strong in their conviction of their yearning flee before the fire and the blaze of an emancipated revelation. When the mind has once been injected with patterns of thought, and these patterns of thought that put the mind in abeyance are accepted, that is when the outcome of your struggle with the affirmation, "I have a right not to be negative," comes to be tested. It is seldom met when personality is on the field! *The personality is always struggling for supremacy, because the genetic handouts of a false mothering and fathering have created such a "false-identity package."* That which has sprung out of the womb is filled with expectancy, but is misidentified in its aptitude to be allowed to enunciate with discipline and guidance gradual victory over its new medium or new atmosphere of experience.

To be reborn means that something has to die. What part of "you" has to die? There is no part of "you" that has to die. All of "you" has to! Who ever heard tell of part of "you" watching the other part bury it?! All of "you" has to die. [laughter] Why is it such a laughable matter? It is your resistance and release of energy at the thought of relinquishing your hold on *an identity of comfortability* which appears because you are surrounded by the likes of those dressed for this Earth masquerade.

Thanksgiving for what? **For the wonder that death is appearing as life!** The very nature at our feet, before our eyes, springs vitally ever new to our sense of the colorful passage of leaves, of flowers, and of fruit. This does not mean that it is dying but that it is regaining the strength that is essential to birth newness in the correct season of man's sequential expectations.

The purpose of recognizing the wonderfully rhythmic nature and the intervallic nature of even objective life points to something to be discovered. That something to be discovered is that which bestows freedom to face the suggested unfruitful situation with the *knowing* that if the seed is planted in fertile soil and watered and nurtured, it will bear fruit according to its kind. This is why, when you have the willingness to align yourself to What IS not dying, you can allow it to appear to happen and you start to understand "Be ye present with Me as I AM, and let the dead bury the dead."

This is how we attend unto the autumn of time, for we know that in the disintegration of the system of belief is the evidence of the integrating force of the all-consuming, all-pervasive, and all-encompassing power of Love's freedom.

> *What is the power of Love's freedom?*
> *The constant presence of volition in perfect*
> *balance with passivity or the condition of*
> *reception.*

*What is the mark of a called-out one if it is not in **the recognition of immediate acceptance of what you do not understand**. Nothing can be revealed of a higher nature to the intellect via understanding. The higher is revealed only through experience. You will find that one of the greatest* secrets of all time is that which is wrapped in the garment of experience. Experience is *never outward;* experience is *always internal.* The part that appears outward only after the experience has fulfilled itself is your ability to expound with "understanding" the invisible meaning of the growth of wonder of the invisible realm.

Understanding reveals itself with a teacher who can say that two plus two is *known* to be four to the child who *thinks* it five. The knowing condition of the teacher is known for fact because the understanding is present in the face of an assumption that two and two is five. It is understanding that allows itself to be considered so valuable. Why? It is not understanding a theorem or any expression of symbolic nature that is of immense importance; it is the understanding that allows one to perceive the viable nature of the non-manifested, for it is the divine attraction to your pyramid of intellectual stones. These must become the stepping stones of your freedom, not the evidence of your structure of misunderstood, not-understood rooms filled with the mystery lost because of the reluctance to practice, in seclusion, Being present and living in two worlds at the same time!

The mystery of the pyramid is always contemplated. Do you suppose that the pinnacle of its attainment is the experience of being freed from the embodiment and finding how to live, in simplicity, as the spiritual colossus and have your stride in two worlds, successfully fulfilled by the enunciation that everyone has the choice not to be negative? Practice it and see that the choice to be positive is the only condition that reduces the negative. Then "you" are reduced, and being reduced, you are committed to understanding the Key because you are now at the point where you are simple enough to penetrate the lock to the door that opens upon the other World at will.

Why is the Key, Identity, important? *It is because the true Identity fundamentally has nothing whatsoever to do* *with the pattern of intellectual thought-structures associated with your personality. Identity has to do with accepting those thought-structures that are known to be constant because they come from the realm of the limitless.*

The only limit anyone experiences is due to the belief system surrounding probabilities. "It is probable that you will all be successful if you work, but it is also known that the probability of everyone achieving the highest is limited because of the lack of jobs, because of the lack of sufficient expertise on the certain levels of the highest attainment." *This is inaccurate!*

> **There is no limit to your attainment but what you set as "the limit" of your energy and willingness to scrub the decks of your mind and free it of the encrustations of the belief systems of ages!**

This is not a frivolous enunciation surrounding Thanksgiving for a harvest of nature's natural bestowals. *It is a Thanksgiving for those who would understand the wonders of seeding your fertile ground of yearning with the perennial knowledge of the ground of Being!*

Freedom is what is experienced when you have freed yourself from the false thought-structures surrounding "you." You are not a human being; *you are Being appearing human.*

We have adopted and have adapted through the willingness to crush the herbs of suggestion to find the fragrance of the Sage an intrinsic part of our own seasoning. We all bear that quality that will entice those who ask for "Food, Sahib!" with *the fragrance of Presence* that is freed from the stench of slow death.

When you are with people who are bemoaning their state, if you would stop your thought-association and perceive it as the verbal stench of an ensuing death, you would not be party to such an encounter and would involuntarily start doing the work of correct Identification within yourself in order to bless the one who is parading a false identity in thoughts.

Your work is not to free yourself in death and still live for selfish purposes; it is to free yourself so that others may see that *a purpose is only the preliminary requirement to evidencing the wonder of internal experience with the outward glow of a radiance commensurate with the adoption that becomes a ray of Stardom!*

There is no one in this world that is born without a ray. The outer garment is of little consequence if the inner one is not spotless. You must find your robe spotless and "white as the driven snow," for you are in the presence of the Invisible and yet visible. *Without the seeming agreement to be visible, the Invisible would not be known to be able to have a contact with your realm of supposition. To the Invisible the suppositional is only an aroma befitting the needs of those who are willing to crush the suggestion of a false life experience.*

What experience have you to give to another at your present state if it is all wrapped up with "you"? The tendency of people to-day is to create a "couch potato" society, totally mesmerized by the boob-tube, totally expanding because of potatoes! No longer do people suffer from "chips off the old block"; they suffer from greasy potato chips from potatoes that never had a chance to bear more than the eyes in the mud! You do not have the eyes to see that a chip of a potato gives you nothing but a taste, but a chip off the old block should enable you to realize that a wooden head is only for splitting the intellectual logs of limitation!

Why have you patience with the rumors that you are "this"? **Rejoice in the wonder of being Love radiating involuntarily!** *Who cares* but societies who have refused to look after their own child-like thoughts, and thus you see the children needing care. Do not blame it on the children! The children are there to satisfy your selfish nature. Perhaps without your knowing it, the child is desired to give you confidence that Life does go on from the Invisible because out of it comes your wondrous child. But if you do not see that the child is *the evidence* of the continuing link of man's at-Onement with divinity, how can you satisfy one another? You are all children, but now the only things you need to have changed are the diapers of your mind!

People make such messes, for they think that logic is what should prevail. Logic is the midway point in our scale for educational purposes. Below is paranoia; above is *metanoia*. No one knows what metanoia is, so I am told; no one has ever been able to speak of it, so I am told. It is obvious that if no one has been able to speak of it, it is because in the logical mind it is only known to exist, not understood! So you have to work with those who are paranoid!

Who are the paranoid? They are on the next level above the animal, vegetable, and mineral. Do you wish to remain so close to being the vegetable? Many do, and you see people ending their lives devoid of any form of intellectual cohesiveness.

What is essential? **Freedom!** It is not the freedom of races; it is not the freedom of governments; it is not the freedom that you put into the object. *Freedom is the releasement from the realm of intellectual chaos, which will allow you to permeate the field with the seeds that will bear a crop of radiance! It is far-fetched, yet here it is at hand!*

If you are just reaching middle age, as Zsa Zsa Gabor said, "There comes a time when it is either your face or your fanny!" It is obvious that both are setting-in, and you had better consider what it is that comes after U/"*you*"! Z has to do with Zsa! V does not have to do with the Victoria Falls; it has to do with *the victory that others perceive as you are emancipated from your false identity and its constant crises.*

People say, "I cannot speak easily to Mr. Mills." Of course, you cannot! You are complex; I AM simple. How does "a complex," sentenced to complexity, ever understand simplicity? The complexity never gives you uniqueness. *The mark of the emancipated is uniqueness;* it is not a pleasing, magnetic personality. It is the simple, by its presence, involuntarily making the rugged places plain and the high Way accessible without the need of detours.

All the Teachings that are appearing in books to-day are bearing a language similar to this in some ways. The only thing one has to be aware of is: *The language may appear to be the same, but if it has no **altering effect in sound,** it has paucity within its nature!*

The penurious of mind will never be able to understand the plenitude of the Invisible!

Now, you may say, "How does all this unusual word-formation, given to us in sound and shaken from the Life-Tree, bear meaning to this moment?" *Your presence witnesses in these very words the practicality, because it is a **moment to moment bestowal.*** It never ceases, even when it is said to be hell or heaven! This is your intellectual framework of reference for dissonance or harmony. Neither is known nor considered in the Invisible. *Heaven and hell are dramatized or "costumized" by being "customized" for those "culturized" by being "civilized" in the atrocities of the mind!* Why are they the atrocities of the mind? *Because you are not taught to discriminate the thought-patterns and find them pertinent unto the very God of Light and Love and bearing the fire of transformation!*

You cannot be empowered by the divine and speak with a voice that would put you to sleep! People used to say to me, "Why do you speak in such high light in a room?" I said, "Because I never speak in the subdued lights if you think the subdued lights are going to let you gain more."

The high Light is so bright that it will blind you if you see it, as it did Moses! Yet the bush was not consumed, do not forget! What is the bush? It has remained a mystery for centuries. *Perhaps the bush that was not consumed was the one that bore the leaves of wisdom and the healing power to the nations of thought precipitated as cultures!* This is why any bigotry or bias of color, race, and creed is such a detriment to the wonders of a universal harmony!

This is the practicality! This is the wonder! Not this off-pitch business or this raucous sound that does nothing but torment. All rock-and-roll should be banned, because it forces upon the ear the sounds that are chaotic and purely emotional.

> **The emotional nature is there for a reason.**
> **What is that reason?**
>
> **It allows you to yearn . . for unity!**
> **It is the eternal movement under the law of**
> **the divine magnet of Love.**

Love sets the captive free, but it does not tell you that the captive *is* free because the captive has been taken in the net of Love's fullness! That is human Being, being human, human Being, being human . . *freed!* Unbound!

> **Why is the *Feeling of Being* essential?**
>
> **It is the only rarefied emotion**
> **that bridges the Invisible and the visible.**

The reason it is said to be associated with the Synonym of *Soul* is because it cannot be contaminated, it is so far beyond the intellect of siege. It is never conquered; it is never lost. *It is the very foundation of your yearning to Be — That!*

The reason the Soul is structured is because
it is the only Synonym of God that can be
"thought" into a vessel. And it displaces just
enough on the surface of the sea of
Consciousness so that it sails on the inspired
breath of the wind into the enchanted
land of enhancement of the divine, for
the rudder is under the hand of a clearly
defined intention.

They say practice makes perfect. (Do not tell the children that it does not!) It is not practice that makes
perfect; *it is practice that allows you to perceive how much
of "you" is in the way!* The reason we do abstract exercises
is so that we can "destroy" anything that would hinder our
attempted worship of the divine; in other words, "we" are
not destroyed through our attempted worship if our
intention is right. *If your heart is right, there is a song of
gladness even in the darkest night!*

Why would you say, "In the Light I see Light" (Do
you?) and "In the darkness I see it not"? If you perceive
darkness, the Light is present! If you perceive Light, you
have to verify it, because there is such a mechanical, counterfeit nature of light to-day that unless man is found aligned
to Principle, *not person* ("me," or "anyone" else), he is
under false tutelage. *Your tutorials should come to an end if
you are not being taught that Principle is fundamental.*

This is the value of perception: What is not perceived is
what is waiting to be perceived, to evidence your skill of
overview or purview! *You have to have an overview in order
to get out of yourself.*

I read this to-night, to my utter amazement: *"The last
words of the Magnum Opus of the Initiate: True initiation
is a process of unfoldment."* When you rehear an
Unfoldment™ you are being allowed, once again, through

the grace of the Word, to hear what your errant, erratic, intellectual thought-patterns prevented you from hearing the first time, and you call it "rehearing."

Do we not live under the most incredible evaluation? We live on compliments. When you do not compliment, there is nothing attractive to be around. No one comes to be freed of compliments. If you are not complimentary, there is no pass into your audience chamber! Do you know why? You have such a lack of *confidence.*

They tell us in the old approach, "Blessed assurance! Jesus is mine! O what a fortress! Such a glory divine!" Words of salvation? What is to be saved? That which is already dying? What is to be salvaged? What remains hidden as a result of yearning. *Yearning always reveals an unfulfilled state which is a blessing in disguise; it is the evidence of the higher Self giving you a way to feel the unity, the Oneness, a viable unitary Principle, universally inclusive and cosmically endowed with the fructifying power of unlimited creative potential!*

Do you think you are going to have it one minute if you constantly alter your state of a moment-to-moment wonder — a wonder that *salt, water, chalk, protoplasm, or slime, all slung together in a bag in time* is able to contemplate and meditate on the Invisible? The Invisible is known to exist when thought ceases to interrupt, thus reducing the suppositional evidence of "thinker"! The value of meditation is the moments experienced freed from "you," the thinker, and you are present with the wonder of your invisible fortress that is termed God, the Source, the Energy. *This is why the great Exemplar, Jesus, is always termed such a fortress, for He withstood the siege of the intellectual minds to try to make the invisible Law viable in the sight of the biased law of limitation.*

What is the value of the Law of the Prophets if it did not evidence a fatidic splendor? Why is a fatidic splendor so enticing? Because men and women in civilization generally live on the edge of expectancy. Unless you are yearning, you have no idea what to expect. How can you expect water from a well that has gone dry?

In this day and age, how can you expect to receive anything from a society that has lost the wonder of artistic endeavor and classical attainment? What is necessary? The silencing of noise. What is also necessary, as I said twenty-seven years ago, is the return to the schoolroom of those who sponsor children and parents. If parents are expectant, have built their nest, and are waiting for the wonder to arrive, they can be taught not only how to take care of the child but how to let the child intuitively feel the nurturing experience without the intellectual interference of patterns. The child bears forth its own need! Let the mother ask only when she cannot stop the whimpering. A whimper always suggests a need. The child, having none until *you* saw it, whimpers now on your level of awareness; it whimpered not in its sea, for it was rhythmic, and it kicked in rhythm with the heartbeat of the support system.

What part of you is kicking in rhythm with your Heart rhythm? Have you ever considered the tender, delicate nature of a divine Idea, waiting in its gestation period to birth, experienced? The change is evidenced by your growth in grace, distilling the perspiration of fear and terror and lack by the presence of understanding so that it may appear as dew upon the rose in your garden in the dawn's early light!

*Your projection unto your time and unto your space demands the newness of moment-to-moment, not the refuse of planned activity. It demands **the spontaneous response to the moment of Presence.*** Your school systems have to be rebirthed and the teachers have to *experience* in secret so that they will know what words to utter as food to the new, young things of time, for they shall be fed and fly according to their inheritance.

Your system in schools is disintegrating because there is no integration with Principle, which is not thought. Principle is only a thought until known, and then it reveals not a thinker but one who knows how to empower the Now! The k-n-o-w has the *K*, the power of the Invisible. The electrical force-field empowers the *Now* through knowing! That is how it is *won*, because in the reflective spirit, n-o-w in the mirror is w-o-n. This is how, as your understanding gives you the hickory stick, your experience reflects what appears so essential to the future!

We are in a sequence of events that the robotery of the minds has precipitated into activity that will destroy the very existence of most "space suits." We are at what is termed fatidically "the end of the century." That is how time has been marked by prophets. Prophets have tried to put the timeless into time in order to be able to offer something to bide the moments until each can be fecundated with the presence of the Invisible manifesting in the Now. This is a time of such force because there is going to be a coincidence. That coincidence is frightening because men have dreamed vainly that something *new* will happen in 2000!

What is your only alternative to this vise of coincidence? The crush of wisdom and its un-utilization? Or the *bearing* of wisdom, which will give Light unto your feet and allow you to walk the corridor between parallel centuries? They are octaves apart, and your only freedom, if you have *gained it,* is by the right of obedience to the Law of Love, Truth, and Life.

Personality will be crushed, for it has nothing to offer. The marks of the Great have never ceased to exist, for the Record is not made by hands; it is a force that imprints, upon the birthing cognition of something lacking, the ingredient that is essential for that Soul's achievement and its emancipation from false identity.

It does not matter whether you understand this or not. How could "you"?! If "you" are thinking, you will understand nothing, for this is not thought. I AM no thinker. *All you have to do is experience by witnessing and accept by your inner motivation to fulfill yearning. The terror that pervades this planet is a result of agreement to sponsor a counterfeit existence.*

My number of days of speaking to you is not known, but I have said enough that you will have no concern *ten thousand years from now* if you follow it. Socrates and Pythagoras said the same things over a thousand years ago. Jesus is closest to most of you and to me; He is just a short time ago. Even closer to Jesus was Buddha, and even closer to Jesus, on the other side, was St. Francis. But what is the use of a name if it does not call you to attention, for each one precipitated on your invisible Scroll a possibility of satisfaction when releasement from *what-you-are-not* was adopted and you adapted to the Path of the "Lonely Ones."

You can throw out your masquerade, all your costumes, but do not throw the child out with the water. *Do not throw away the idea of wonder just because elegance prevails. Do not throw away the idea of wonder when poverty prevails.* Just know that each is an appearance in a sequence of holy events, bearing for you the needful activity of involuntarily bestowing your gift of your silent experience. *The Silence is fructifying each moment of your apparent human incarceration with the wonders of unfettered Being.*

*There is **nothing** to interfere with the rhythmic pulsation of a divine intention and its natural, unlimited fulfillment.* From looking at the form, how do you know the wonder that has allowed it to appear so beautiful or so ugly? There is not a mistake. *Perhaps you thought you could get away and flee from the Truth of Being,* and then find not the awareness or the understanding when you desire to take on another coat of form; then you do not understand your blindness, your deafness, your lameness, the missing limb, your crippled body! Always give help, but *never* from the standpoint of being a do-gooder. Give help from the standpoint of the allness of God-Being. Keep out of it personally, because you will never understand the formations which confront you, for you do not know the *nature* of the invisible Soul factor that is at work in structuring the essential vehicle and its qualities in order to understand wonder!

Do you have confidence? It is only known by the experience. You cannot wear jewelry and you cannot say, "I love gold, I love jewelry, I love. Behold!"[1] if you have not the confidence of Reality as your bosom experience.

You expect unity to arrive upon your experience by thinking in terms of binary: right, wrong; good, bad; I have, you have not; she is beautiful, he is ugly. The binary enters not in the sight of an eagle! *Fly high as the eagle.* What have sheep to do with flight?[2] Sheep are the symbol of thoughts. *There is not a poem that has come from the "foyer of wonder" that has not borne the tantalizing fragrance of the wonders of the Other Side.*

Why are you so cast down and so disquieted within, if it is not a personal attempt to be holy when you have not surrendered to the allness of Love's ministrations?! Love is not some ooey-gooey force of attraction. It is the Power behind the hickory-stick and it is the Power that disciplines. Through practice, perception is perceived as changing.

> How do I view? How do I see?
> God? Man? "You" and "me"?
> How do *I* view? How do *I* see?

---

1. See "I Love Jewelry. I Love Gold," a poem by K. G. Mills, *The Golden Nail* (Stamford/Toronto: Sun-Scape Publications, 1993), p. 350.

2. "The Eagle," K. G. Mills, *Embellishments* (Toronto: Sun-Scape Publications, 1986), p. 103.

None other but *I*, and you see me!

You yearning to BE and I hearing the plea,
Appearance appeared appareled in deed.
In doing, in Being, in evidence,
        in sight/insight,
The bridge was created for a Soul's delight.

Over it walk with the invisible feet,
Knowing That salvation. Pleading *weak?*
Knowing Be! Find the balm
That heals the wounded and shields from
        harm.

For the moment shall come to those bowed
        with care,
Provided the heart is strong and the desire
        prayered.
The prayer of those bound never goes
        unanswered, you know,
For a prayer transcends the thinker's shore.

Prayer unbound gives to the human scene
The wonder of a *hue* and *Man* beyond your
        dreams,
For the man of knowing becomes like the
        symbol at hand:
A diamond, a fire, transparent on hand.

Transparent Stone and transparent Man —
        ah!!
Visible, yet invisible.
How do "you" know I AM?

A Verbologist's Wonder is the dance
To the invisible, unheard Music which exists
        beyond trance!

Where is a "you" when I AM found?
Wrapped up in victory, or plummeting to
    ground?

**What an amazing grace to perceive
the insignificance of suggestion
and the magnitude of Truth!**

▼

Chapter XIV

Are Ye Not Gods?

confidence

blessings/gratitude

new birth

silver cord

unlimited possibilities

Power of Tonality

Great Verbology

Unity

Are Ye Not Gods?

We are gathered together to count the blessings. We count our blessings in order to prove to ourselves that we have an ability of consecutive thought that does bear possibilities when it is used correctly. The actuality of numbers is not that they breed anything new; they just allow you to perceive what you have not used, a sequential order of probabilities that are beyond numbering.

The essential characteristic of gratitude is that it is unlimited. We cannot number the blessings that are bestowed upon us, for they are so great that even in our ignorance, our stupor, our lethargy, and our indolence, they allow the experience of seemingly being different after they have stilled the contemptuous mental realm of its control-promptings to dwarf the magnificence of the unlimited Source of our Being.

It is under the aegis of this great Unknown that men question the state that is so apparently binary. We are so apparently governed by the binary concept that it begins in the very fundamentals of numbering: day and night, right and wrong, good and bad, men and women, "haves" and "have-nots," know-it-all and know-it-nothing! *The binary form constitutes the bracelets, the matching bracelets of bondage!* Nothing can happen by two. Two only exists in your numerology as the evidence of co-operation with One! That in itself is the clue to the harmonic structure that is ever waiting to be experienced universally. For it is within the realm of the considerations being proffered unto people to-day that the opportunities of the future (that men dream as a result of binary, sequential considerations) are opportunities of bearing freedom not only from the past and its darkness but the future and its dismal nature.

Consider the moments in which you find yourself present: If they are not filled with the unlimited bestowal that is accepted as a blessing beyond all counting, then you are not able to perceive all that could be happening in the name of the One altogether lovely and the rescinding of the concept of multiplicity, all given back to the undifferentiated and yet experienceable Source of the vibrational frequency of creative might.

If God is in His temple and all is right with the world, another way of saying it is that "God is sounding my Beingness, and my temple radiates with the vibration of the bell struck by acceptance." You are the structure of the very living Presence, and that is why sometimes it is said, "Ye are gods." Why are you gods? Because by acceptance and willingness you can drop the contaminated and broken cast of a humanoid and find yourselves bearing "the costumization" of formation that is really a camouflage for the upright tonality of Being present! This is termed *"a reverberation of wonder"* in the annals of time, and those who have radiated this wonder have been termed "the Greats" of our belief in an historical past and a promising future.

You cannot have the existence of an historical past if you are not already "goal-ized" to a future. *Binary action is always limited action that goes nowhere but to an end.* There is no repetition to a binary action; it is dead. It sprang from a belief that God could divide Himself, or that the

Father-Mother Ideal is divisible into parts. That is a suggestion of your mind, but the goal is to have all the parts fitly joined together. What a panacea for the deluded! What an offering for the mathematically-minded to try to bring together the parts so that they are fitly joined together, *when it is only the mind's improbable nature toward sincerity that has destroyed the unity from the beginning!* You were never cast into parts; you were the totality of Being as Idea, uncontaminated and unfettered by the belief of uterus, wombing, and birthing.

The perverted concept of a mind is fretful as a result of its *partial* knowledge of What IS and what is not! This is why we are so inclined and so encouraged to be indoctrinated with education. We are inclined to be kicked from the past into the future by getting a degree of acceptance in our mediocrity by the very professorship of a limited chair of action. It cannot turn in any direction; it is stayed at a table *not* laden with the fructifying food of an unlimited palette of wonder. You are caught not in a sequence of holy events but in such a bastardized series of events that the one divine event, known as Love, is not even cognized but bypassed in a gown of talk.

Words without action are a waste of energy. It is wonderful to know that all the waste that is prepared and precipitated upon this plane is not other than a concept of the mind, which, somewhere within the recesses of its darkness, knows that **it is a sin to waste the holy Breath by appearing to ejaculate words that are nothing but the sawdust of a vocabulary of mediocrity!**

It is said you are endowed with rights, but how can you know what rights are when they are based on binary considerations? There is no right to be God; there is no right to be presiding over God's kingdom; there is no **right!** *There is only one activity that is termed God-ing, Love-ing, Truth-ing, Being, Mind-ing, Soul-ing, Principle-ing, Son-ing, Spirit-ing.* The Synonyms of God are never left to an imperfect resonator! This is why we know there is more to the sound than we usually hear, because *we do not bear the resonating chamber of a foyer of unalterable service and wonder.*

We are a universal force, engendered and dramatized and dynamized to thrill on the possibilities of accenting those notes of such significance that they are termed "a trill of our lives!" We are constantly jubilating over the exigencies of spiritual import; we are spiriting those energies to the visibility of reception so that they may be cognized as the evidence of an artless and yet artful act of unlimited service.

There is no role in this world that is foolproof!

> A Star, it broke the horizon of time
> And it caused a rift in the mentality, the
>   mind.[1]
> If it were not for the Star that took your
>   attention on high,
> How could you come to have to reconsider
>   your humanoid suggestion caught in
>   hide?

You would never have considered "Who am I? What am I?" if a rift in the mentality, the mind, had not been caused. It was the cleft in the rock of the adamantine nature of a humanoid. **Everyone bearing form has a cleft in the rock of suggestion. If it were not for this, there would be no crevice where the humus of infinite possibilities could be found and the seed of** *dedication to finding* **could be planted;** there would be no possibility of a deep enough root, for it would be a superficial indoctrination in dogma with its limiting and unrevivifying activities of a continuing legacy of Light. It would have been a continuing legacy of constrained enthusiasm for the life of Spirit. The essential need of to-day is to find your face radiant, regardless of statements made.

---

1. Kenneth G. Mills, "The Sound of a Star," *The Tonal Garment of The Word* (Sun-Scape Records, KGOC/D33).

What does it matter if you use make-up and you call it pancake make-up? You have really dropped onto the table of perception, anyway! *Why do you consider dressing it up as if you were anything other than what you are: a stand-in for a divine purpose.* As long as the belief of binary is foremost in the considerations of on-lookers, then *the consideration of Oneness must be dressed-up as that vibrancy that a face wears. The face is the canvas upon which the inner qualities and attitudes contained within the formation exude the Life or death throes. It is marked upon the countenance: the dynamism that is still living, or the ember that is slowly dying.*

This you were given upon accepting the three-dimensional experience: **the magic of being able to consider beyond what you thought!** You were able to consider that your mind was not complete because it could not answer what was not given to it.

Numbering is nothing but an attempt to allow you to perceive with the dexterity of your mind that you can multiply, subtract, and divide with the greatest of ease, even without your lap-top! The world of commerce and finance is being so ruled by the overlapping of time-space sequences that we are dwindling our very legitimate sense of progress because we are not experiencing a contest of inventive wonders; we are trying to beat each other at the game of getting the perishable as much as possible, as if it, instead of our God-Essence, were permanent substance.

The whole value of any contest is so that we can do what? Hopefully, you have been taught what to do. You have been taught *to be able to pace yourself in any contest and see how you are achieving in comparison with those who have a like disposition for your chosen field of expression.* Instead of that, we say one is greater, one is less; what we should be saying is, "Oh, I see in your evidence my possibilities!"

When I used to go to concerts and hear great artists, Rubinstein and Casadesus and Horowitz and Gina Bachauer,

I did not say, "Oh, my God, those are my contestants!" I said, "They are the evidence of my unlimited possibilities!" *Are you saying that about what you perceive? Or are you saying, "Why can't we have this? He's got it. Why can't we have that car? I want that car, just like he's got. What does he need of it? If he hasn't got money, why isn't he driving a Volkswagen, so that he could put it in my trunk so that I could feel a greater sense of self-esteem?"*

There is nothing more debilitating than trying to achieve a sense of self-esteem by dishonoring your likeness! There is nothing more enervating than to compress because of a lack of confidence. **Your lack of confidence only comes because you have refused to accept the Key, Identity! You refuse to adopt the attitude of the dynamism that activates your puppets. You are all puppets on the string of mind instead of the string of vibration constituting the silver cord/chord of universality so that all others may hear the tonality, the resonance when that string is sounded by the agreement to be other than this human, annoyed at the attainment of his brothers and sisters!**

Do not judge the weary and the cast down and the starving. Give help to those who have been deprived, but do not adjudicate. You do not know the Laws that are in activity as a result of the denial of a God of Light, of the denial of a Teacher of Light, the breaking of commitments to the Light. These may constitute the formations that have gathered in one part of the Earth, because *they have to see the parched conditions of refusal, when their service was expected to be utilized in exonerating the suggestion of those who were imbued with guilt.* **There is no guilt, only in the binary, and say, "I refuse the binary because I am *bound* to the rhythm of my God-Being!"**

That is **always** creative! You do not know how, you do not know why! You are so dull because your wits are coming to an end. [The sound of a passing train is heard.] The evidence of binary-ism: two tracks, "I will" and "I won't. But I want to get on." You are going to! You are going on whether you want to or not; there is no elixir found even in Shangri-la! Shangri-la is yours as soon as you dare to go through the mountain peaks of your life created by refusal, lack of responsibility and commitment to the Light Way of the continuing presence of the eternal ember of Light's radiance.

In the great moving picture that was caught on celluloid about Shangri-la being found behind this mountain range, you will notice (if you ever looked at the old movie), the people have a guide whom they follow, and, if they do not, they are destroyed. They have to pass through the frozen and slippery conditions, the treacherous conditions of snow, pointing to the incredible winds that sweep your crystallized thoughts into drifts that are almost impassable because of your refusal to *become as a sunbeam upon the windowsill of time*. Pass through those drifts of mental formations! Allow the obdurate nature to melt in the presence of a fragrance of a Rose, and allow the Self.

What are you looking for? Do you know the news? You have been hooked! *What you are looking for, you have been taught you lost.* That is why you had to be given so much education, to make it more difficult to learn that you did not lose anything! You were taught that you had lost it, so that the mind could control your inalienable rights as gods. Who wants to hear this message? Few. You all go out in the world and behave in your way, instead of taking your world up and walking through its byways and renaming all the streets, all the avenues, and seeing the wonder of those places that exist beyond the Port of Despair, the Port of Hope, or Blissville.

Go beyond the Port of Hard Knocks and go beyond the Port of Doubt! Why stop? When your train of thought ceases, you get off at that point that becomes the very vibrating center and circumference of your experience, for you have not screwed yourself up into a timid budhood but you have allowed yourself to extend the petals of your wonder and reveal the unlimited possibilities that are entrenched as yours within the Scroll of Light.

You would never have been given this experience if it were not expected for you to have remained contrite, filled with integrity to your initial prompting to **find an authentic Nature.** This is your prime, aboriginal beginning. It was to find verbology the ultimate on this level. It has to do with the great verb "To BE" and the "-ology" surrounding it! This is the Great Verbology, because the verbs that are used, the words that are used, never bear the ending, "to be or not to be?"

The registration is divine! All the pipes speak according to the theme that is present and required for the service of a tonal engagement. The great organ is a perfect symbol of what our resources should be, the bellows not necessarily pneumatically operated but electrically *charged,* and the pipes attuned to *"I love wondrous Tonality!"* The registration of a program for a festival of Sound is not haphazard. You spend hours taking the internal spectrum of sound and finding the corresponding identity in the ranks of pipe that constitute the great organ, and naming them in order to call upon them, and then giving them to a general piston, so that the registration can be changed instantaneously for the newness of expression. It is done with the feet and it is done with the thumb. You can be playing on many keyboards, and your thumbs automatically know where to go below the key levels to alter the tones as you are playing. You dance with your feet as you do with your fingers, and your thumbs are taught to do what they cannot think to do! Do not think of thumbing your way and hitchhiking in spirit!

The Spirit is to Be the Way so that another will follow and find upon completion that the guide left no footprints; they only seemed to be there to give him confidence, for his assurance was not secure enough for his passage. *Confidence comes from the experience, not from talking about experimental, philosophical, metaphysical lectureship!* It is the experiential that is the need of to-day, and your study should find just how much approving you need even to be here! You are obviously so dammed in your thought that you do not realize you have dammed! It is bigger than the Hoover Dam, for *the "God-dam" is made-up of the concrete of obstinacy and willfulness all based on personal self-aggrandizement, instead of the intention to self-abnegation* and you become a virtuoso in the realm of Verbology, not one bearing vituperation in the language of an intellectual ass!

Harassment! This is what you do with the incorrect language. Have you ever thought men were harassed as much as women? You do not have to have the visible action when your mind-thoughts or the thoughts of your mind are so digitalized that they spread out in an invisible web and trip you into limitations! What are your races, colors, and creeds other than an attempt to hold the binary in some form of disciplined position until a technique is arrived at. Practice does not make perfect, but practice allows a scheduling of events of constancy so that the utilization of these abstract moments develops a worthwhileness. In the seclusion of your aloneness, there is developed the mastery that allows the Self to express itself. You no longer stumble upon the keys surrounding your complexes but you are registered to know the One great piston upon which you stand and thus ejaculate the tones of wonder commensurate to the grand organ and perhaps the grand Man of the universe of Light!

These are the words that bring to a close these moments of exploration and adventure as we have lifted the veils and the skirts of belief and revealed that the peak of attainment is not to be found other than in the evaporation, in the heat of the present nowness of Being. Find that all the thought-structures of an incorrect identity lie as ashes bearing the fragrance of the Rose, for you never faltered in transcending the thorns of belief. You never doubted that the screwed-up bud, grounded in the cleft of the rock of unshakable Truth, would bear root and blossom. You know that the ashes of roses bear the fragrance that even the living body did not offer until its greatness appeared as death! It lives, either you would not bear the Fragrance, you would not know the Fragrance, and you would not wear the Fragrance. It has nothing to do with a history of men and women; it has to do with the perpetual wonder of the rhythm of cosmic significance surrounding the thrill of Life. You have seen the continuing trill of ornamentation appearing as this lectureship and appearing as these very tonalities, all strung on your rosary of attention and proclaimed, adorning the universe of possibilities with a one world given back to the arms of Love!

Thank you for your flowers; thank you for your gifts; thank you for the presence in which we find ourselves in the same pattern, in the same field of Light and wonder, in the proclamation that *"I know whom I have chosen."* You who have heard, **are ye not gods when released from a false identity of this mortality and its trends?**

▼

I am not this earthen body of clay.
I AM Conscious-Being!

Chapter XV

Passion

passivity

me/mine

attention

birth/death

divine intention

oral Transmission

essence

I AM

Principle

Passion

We have gathered the riches from the Cache that is retrievable for you at this time. It is caught in the pages of memory, it is caught in the symbolic nature of symbols as words and diagrams, but it is also known to live only when it is orally transmitted, for the symbol bears not *the awakening power of tonality*. The awakening power of tonality is such that upon hearing a sound, one's attention is taken.

If one's attention is taken, and one perceives that the attention *is* taken, is it not readily obvious that one should be on guard as to *what takes the attention?* As we have all perceived in our visitation to time, unkind words, negative statements, responses, and attitudes take the attention more readily and are more easily remembered than those that attain a prominence by being "in keeping with a higher modus operandi."

When we entertain words, we give our attention to watching and to hearing a number of them, and the number of them either conforms or does not conform to what we have deemed commensurate or in keeping with the comfortability of our thought-network.

When the oral Transmission is given that is in keeping with what you have been considering, give your attention to it until you get tired of hearing something you have already given your attention unto! Suddenly, you realize a fascinating point: When the attention is taken by a Verbalization, it is held to the extent that the intellectual *cognition* of the statement has become more than an intellectual statement. You realize that it has become a fundamental characteristic of experience.

An intellectual statement that does not *live* soon *tires* the attention. This is why your attention seems to be yours, because you are responsible for utilizing that focused point to bring into proximity what you are attuned unto that will allow you, as a conscious experience, to be freed from what you are *not*.

We have so mistaken activity as being the evidence of our agility in scaling the octaves of intellectual discernment and explanation. You can hear a thing said and you can expand upon it and expand upon it, but unless you have contracted the expanse to the point where it is penetrating the veil that confronts you as otherness, and offering a blessing, you are doing nothing but polluting the atmosphere with energy of which the "opposition" will gladly make use.

The energy that you do not use is utilized elsewhere! The energy cannot be wasted because there is nothing but energy! The suggestion that there is no energy is the suggestion that you have veiled yourself; in other words, you have retreated from the active engagement of ministering Love. You have concealed the purpose of your Intention.

Everyone's path is marked, sometimes through the superficial engagement of a profession, which always evidences itself in attainment and a paycheck. How many ever check what *is* the dividend paid by a profession that does not exemplify the professional's attainment, not only in the art of drawing-upon his intellectual accomplishments but in transcending the limits of that accomplishment so that newness may appear?

If you constantly grind out the old ideas dressed-up in new colors or in a new fabric, you are not keeping in rhythm with the divine glamour commensurate with the style becoming constant newness! "Oh," people say, "be careful of glamour, it will seduce you. Be sure you develop an indifference to everyone (but yourself) and be sure you are detached from everyone (but yourself) and be sure you do not show anyone any generosity (but to yourself) and be sure . . ." But how *can* you be?

"Be sure" was never part of an assertion. The assertion is always from the Standpoint of the most approachable attribute in this Age: **Principle**. The other attributes are fine, but those other attributes or Synonyms of the Source are wrapped up with what we have gleaned in the realm of our religious indoctrination.

Principle is a sound that we are all aware of but seldom conform to! Principle is the root of honesty, and honesty is evidenced as Principle in action. How often is honesty present? It is usually honesty up to the point where one is put into the shadow of not wanting to reveal the honest situation of not knowing, not being able to say "So help me, God!"

To be able to say "So help me, God!" is being honest when you know that you *do not know* what you pretend to know. *Principle is a living stand of vibrating Light! It is the very Center of activity because from it exudes the entire seed kingdom of unlimited possibilities.*

In to-day's world we are given considerations of aptitude in dealing with conflicting ideas. We are given such aptitude that a conflicting idea does not bother us! A *conflicting* idea is one that can *inflict* pain upon you, but you are so psychologically deadened to what it is empowering that you accept it.

How often do you hear a siren? (Forget about those that require you to be roped to the sail. I do not mean those! There are enough of them as it is, but to-day they are not on cliffs.) Think of the sirens that hoot and take your attention. What are they saying? "Pull over" or "There's an emergency." You cannot accept that, if you are involuntarily the servant of your professed Path. You have to know *instantly* that there is no accident in divine Mind, for Principle cannot be harmed or touched in any way. If an accident could happen to God, what hope have you to be freed from the accident of fatal indoctrination and fatal wrong identification?!

Wrong identification is the core of our problems in the world to-day. What is to-day's world? Yesterday's world dressed-up in the continuing episodes of the fashion of relating intervals of questionable significance! An interval is the distance between two tonalities. It is also the distance between periods of historical intent, and it is also the distance that we put between ourselves and the Self. *The interval is the distance that we create to protect ourselves.*

One of the features emblazoned upon our agenda of to-day is the transcending of the suggested *depression*. The *depression* is what you have helped bring about. A depression is a suggestion that there could be a different level of Being from the fullness that is commensurate with allness. *A depression signifies fluctuation; it is part of the dualistic, relativistic, dysfunctional aspects of the path of self-infatuation.*

What is the most important thing you do in the run of the day? Consider yourself! What are you really concerned about from the time you get up until you go to bed? "What will 'me' look like to-day? What will 'me' do to-day? What will 'me' see to-day? How will 'me' be seen to-day? How will 'me' behave to-day? How will 'me' go to bed to-day? Maybe 'me' should not have gotten up to-day. Me's tired already!"

"Me!" is the source of the screaming "me-mes," and they are the cause of the chants of the modern-day contemplative: "Me, mine, yours. Me, mine, yours. Me, mine, mine! Me, mine, mine. Me, mine, mine. Me, mine, yours! Me, mine, mine! Me, mine, yours. Me, mine, mine!" What have you got? *"Me!"* What is the value of a screaming "me"? What type of tonality does *"me"* wear? *"Me"*?

What have you thought about to-day, more than anything else? "I must get my rest. Me is tired! I must not do too much, 'me' has got to be on top to-night . . and on bottom to-morrow." What are we hoping for? A movement of "mes"? What a depression! "Me" is the most oppressive force-field! "Dive deep within," and "me" is trying to breathe! Dive deep without, and "me" is screaming. Whom do you love more than anything or anyone in the world? Not me! *Your* "me"! But if you were Me, you would be I!

The interval between that type of "me" and this type of "I" is such that that type of "me" can scream; this type of *"I" has a constant tonality that represents Keyship and a kinship with the monarchy that is under surveillance to-day.*

What is the symbolic value of a grape leaf? A grape leaf, looked at as a grape leaf, is just a thing. Me, looked at as a "me," is just "me," no-thing, nothing! Why? Because a leaf, or "me," separated, has no life. *A leaf away from the vine has no life.* It seems to live for a short time, and it dries and dies and goes to dust. A "me" separated from the Vine seems to live in the glamour of beautiful clothes, beautiful dinners, beautiful parties, and never for a moment considers the wonder of the vital, dynamic Source that is allowing the festivity to seem to happen. What happens? It dies!

As one writer said, it is like the branch of a tree: A wind has blown very hard and, lo and behold, a beautiful branch is broken off the tree and it falls to the ground. It looks gorgeous, just like the tree, for a little while. In a couple of days (in twenty or thirty years, or three score years and ten), the leaves are aging, they are drying up, they are getting old because the branch, separated from the trunk, has no Source.

This is what a "me" does. It separates from the very vibrant trunk, the Source of Being. If you take a grape leaf and forget not the wonder of the vine, you also know that you have the root system of years and years of assimilating the nutrients of Mother Earth, Gaia, and lo and behold, you have the vine reappearing, with proper pruning, to bear the leaves in preparation for the wonder of the appearance of the fruit of the vine: grapes!

When you see a wonderful cluster of grapes, you see so many of them. The grapes are diversified; there are all kinds of them, all different sizes and shapes and colors. You do not say one grape is better than another grape. You can say one grape is bigger than another grape, but they are all grapes. What makes the unity with the vine important is not the grape, with all its diversity, it is the juice! The other night at class, I gave each one a grape and said, "This is a grape. This is a grape. This is a grape." Blissville, Unionville, Knoxville, Hopeville, "Cantafford," "Tryford," "Sinkstream" — all these different grapes given to all these different places. Port Hope; next stop, Pandora.

Why do you want to *pan* Dora? You should pan Dora and that myth mighty fast, and especially the woman! She did not offer you a grape, she was raging! She was the first mortal woman (it means that she was vulnerable), but look at what she did! She came with a trunkful, a hope chest, filled with all the ills for mankind, because she was so furious that Prometheus had stolen the fire.

How many of you have only the hope of Pandora? What value is it if it goes with a "me"? It becomes the attitude of critics: "We will pan Dora, we will pan Mills, we will pan Schnabel, we will pan Stern, we will pan —" Why pan? Because it carries the myth of revenge when there is no way, or no interest, in claiming the Fire that allows one to articulate the artistry of Being in performance.

The intellectual critic who has never experienced the technical proficiency behind all artistic achievement has to pan, either he reveals he is not capable of performance himself; if he were, he would be subject to his own "panning" operations. Have you ever stopped to consider that a critic who criticizes performance from the standpoint of the intellect is a critic who is destroying the possibility of a divine art emerging, because "me-mes" do not understand the comedy?! They do not understand that this is such a farce because nothing can touch That which is Real. My goodness, when you do not know what IS Real, it seems that all the finest efforts are panned because no one has known how to utilize the scope of a redeemed imagination. This causes the lens to contract until you have only a specific and contaminated "me" viewpoint.

What does Principle give you? The iridescent wonder seen as the variety, the diversified artistic talents, appearing. You can always praise and appreciate, because *when you are freed from the "me," it is only natural to praise, to adore, to serve, and to exalt. If you are not free, all you do is find fault.* There is not a thing wrong with perceiving a fault, provided it is to reveal it to the individual or to the situation so that the situation is free of a fault. Others can say, "There is a miracle."

That is what you call the interval of divine judgment, because judgment should always be given to the Son, and the Son is that awareness of the essence of whatever it is that is appearing. If it is perceived that the sun is shining, then it is also known that the sun fecundates that situation through either suffering or Science, through activity or through nonactivity. The result is that *sooner or later you are forced to perceive what is the Reality to the bifurcated picture.*

It is well to know that when you take a glass of grape juice, the grapes have given up their skin of identity but their essence is imbibed. A grape is never other than a grape.

Why is it that the essence called Man is forgotten when we are faced with the diversified multitude of forms? Essence appears as Conscious-Awareness, and the attention focused reduces the multiplicity to the wonder of the unitary Principle: the Source, the divine Other, the divine or the sacred, or the Root System or the sacred Tree!

We can name it anything we wish, but we have to set it apart from the intellectual jargon if it is going to be efficacious. The divine or the sacred, brought into the language of the mundane or the profane, does not have any power unless you reveal the fact that it must be set apart. This means that **That which IS cannot be considered in the framework of a "me"; it has to be considered as the *Light* to the "me," as the juice is the essence of the grape.** The grape does not think of the juice; the grape is the capsule containing it. It is only when it is crushed through the pressure of wishing essence that essence is found to flow as the blood of the vine.

This is how we bleed for those who do not understand that the common life-giving ingredient is the Blood or the force that is common as an electrical charge. It allows such an incredible consideration to appear manifest as a human or a capsule bearing the instrumentation in a panel called "the mind" and its development called "the intellect."

When we can talk about the mind and the intellect and see how we *can* change them, it is the evidence of What IS, present. You know the Source is right where you thought it was not. When you can say "I don't like 'me' anymore. I'm going to change me. I'm going to change! I tell you I am!" *as long as you think that "I" is a "me," you will never change!* Look at the people who try to change: "I'm going to change. I'm going to lose weight." "I'm going to put on weight." "I'm going to sing." "I'm not going to sing." What is speaking? "Mes," dressing-up their dying, emaciated state by trying to utilize a high-powered name, dropping, you know, "Lady So-and-so, Sir James So-and-so, His Guyship So-and-so." What are you saying? You are name dropping. What do you do? You drop "I" everywhere to try to impress people because you have nothing with which to impress them but an intellect! So when you say "I've got to change," you had better say "*'I' is charge and 'me' will change.*"

I AM Song. "Me" will sing. "Me" has no alternative, because without "I," "me" cannot seem to sustain more than three score years and ten, at the best! Why three score years and ten? Somebody has to limit it, if it is a "me," because *I AM* eternal. *How could I not be eternal if I AM the same in the stories we have just heard, told historically centuries ago by translating the symbols on a page, but only now bearing the fruit of living transmission.*

> **Truth is always the same, yesterday, to-day, and forever, but Truth is not in a sequence of events, even if they are holy. Truth is never in the sequence; Truth is the Light *to* sequence.**

You cannot expect Truth to bear Love's implementation if it is considered lost in a sequence. What appears as a sequential offering of holy events, such as Saints and Sages, Avatars and Selected Ones? If these people appear, it is because the selection is only the way the sequence perceives the appearance. The appearance bears something that is not in the seeming objective confinement. The Light to the sequence is defined in the pithy statement: **I AM THAT I.**

You never can perceive what *I* IS as long as you think "you" will one day. One of the purposes of contemplation is to perceive that you can slow your mind down to such a point that you start to have visions . . and at such other points you need your T-stick![1] When you come out of contemplation, if you are not changed or charged, *I* have never been there. It has just been a practice of gentle mesmerism!

This is why people meditate. They meditate to see that the mind can be altered. It can be started up, it can be stopped, but it never fully stops. If it did, why would you bother picking it up again? I have never seen a Saint or a Sage be other than the body that he said was meditating or contemplating, because as long as he is meditating or contemplating with a body, he has the body that is meditating or contemplating.

---

1. Referring to a **T**-shaped meditation stick used to prop up the head during meditation.

What is the difference? If the Saint or the Sage or the Avatar knows that the Light to the meditation and the contemplation is all there is *to* the meditator or the contemplator, **then the contemplator meditating gives up entering a State. He *is* that State,** because *I* cannot be altered. I *AM* the Altar, I *AM* the activity, I *AM* acting, I *AM* doing, I *AM* Being. Everyone says, "I am *acting,* I am *doing,* I am *being.*" No! I AM . . acting, I AM . . doing, I AM . . Being, I AM . . singing, I AM . . painting, I AM . . loving, I AM . . That. (I "AM-ing" is no longer static as I AM.)

You can see how to take the branch from the tree. You forget to perceive the wonder of the tree if you only look at the branch. You look at someone and say, "I wonder what branch of the tree he came from. I do not know whether that family has a lot of money or not, but if they do, he will inherit so much." Are you going to marry "a branch" or are you going to unite with the Source? *Are you going to persist in trailing after the totality or are you being One with the totality?*

Which came first? Did you perceive the tree or was the tree ready to be perceived? Does it matter which came first? People spend hours wondering which came first, the chicken or the egg. It is an obvious fact that if "the chicken and the egg" is being considered, the Presence came first!

Why are you considering which came first, God or Man? The Silence or the Word? The Sound or the Song? Why are you considering which came first? There was no "first" to be considered. *"First" is the suggestion you have of serializing, and Realization is a perpendicular experience!* It is when all the tonalities line up in a solid chord of fundamentality, and when sung, leave a trace of tone that is satisfying. It can also be jarring, and when it is jarring, it is said to be no longer harmonic but dissonant.

A dissonance does not mean it cannot be resolved; it says, "I am ready to be resolved." Any dissonant situation in time is praying to be resolved. Every dissonant factor in our society, in our world, every aspect of it, is praying to be resolved. This is an opportunity! We all know that the resolution only happens when the Higher is perceived, and we know how the discord must move for resolution. There is no altering the fact that a leading note must rise!

What is a basic dissonance of life? The complex surrounding wrong identification! You wrap yourself in personality, dressed-up in intellectuality, and create dissonance because you assume that your small self is going to use your mask to dissolve itself! It is impossible! The suggested small self *goes* with your "me." This is why the "mes" are always screaming; they have the same force of the erroneous self, or the opposition, in support of them. That opposition is the force-field that has not resolved to BE the divine root and rises as a result of the tension arising from questions regarding identity.

If a thing changes, it *cannot* be Real! That is one of the marks of the *High Teaching,* not the relative teaching. The only purpose of any exercise is to take your attention. The only purpose of any abstract exercise is to show you that there is no obstruction to the intelligence when there is the focused attention. Intelligence operates, and what seems to be an abstract exercise is accomplished. It does not give you freedom, but it does give you the ability to *know* that you can change a belief about a limitation because "you" can become abstracted from the system of belief and utilize it as a means of transcending a belief system of limitation.

Being a pianist, I know all the abstract exercises of Tausig, the volumes of Czerny, the volumes of Philip, the volumes of Chopin, and the Brahms' abstract exercises. Why do you have these exercises? Because they all can lead to a transcendental state. When you once perceive that your attention can be so focused that you can do the impossible in a simple abstract exercise, it means that *anything new can be accomplished if you are willing to adopt wonder and its expectation and sweat as you die in the fire of Translation.*

When I used to practice the abstract exercises, some of which were extremely difficult, I spent two out of five hours of practice a day doing nothing but abstract exercises. The abstract exercises did nothing for what appeared to be my "ability" to experience music, but it was the very ability to focus my attention that allowed me to "die" in performance. I realized, no matter what I put my fingers through, not one of them knew they went through anything!

My little finger did not know it was the thumb, and my thumb did not know it was the little finger! It was my sight misleading me to think that this calcium and this blood, this sinewy appendage called the arm, could be in the same league with the wisdom, the might, the intelligence, that created what appeared as a capsule to satisfy the need for identity.

What is Identity? Not in the thing! Identity is the Light to what *appears* as the thing. When you think the Identity is in the person, you have your personality complexes. When you know that it is the Identity that appears as person, then you realize that it is the *I* that *dents* the depressed state of a false identity and allows one to rise or to transcend the suggestion of this abstraction called Earth and its difficulties.

The Earth difficulties are abstract daily affairs. That is all! Every one of them you are meeting because you have to meet them. It appears that K. G. has the same difficulties in order for you to see how the servant or the janitor has the same difficulties in dealing with the garbage as *you* do! *You* go along collecting it and chasing the collector and wondering what you put out in your garbage so that you can complain about it in your future!

How often are you still complaining about something that somebody said ten years ago?! This shows you what negativity wants: to be kept alive by repetition! *As long as you repeat a lie, you enhance its position and it appears authentic.* Everyone takes this appearance for Real. This is why a Call went out, because unless somebody can come and say it *is not* Real, you believe it *is* Real. It is not Real, because it changes!

Once upon a time, there was one in my life who had made a promise, and I said to him, "You are breaking a promise, and I would seriously consider what you are doing. You have gone to the 'opposition' because of over-identification with your self-infatuation as person and your attainment as a result of knowing One. It could be karmic." The audacity of the "me" said, "If it is, I'll take care of it the next time! I'm going to do what others have done. They have done it and still live; I'll see if I can." I said, "You fool! How do you know that the next time, which you are already dreaming-up, you will have the attention and the awareness to perceive that your blindness or your lamed or maimed condition is a result of the breaking of a promise?" He said, "Well, I've *changed* my mind." I said, *"But that just shows you that what you are depending upon in your life is not Real!" You* cannot change "your" *Mind*. **Mind is changeless.** It seems charged with the holy properties of unity, honesty, faithfulness, fidelity to intention . . because it has none. It IS!

These words are part of our vocabulary and these are the words that must be utilized with regard to Principle — "re-guard" to Principle. You do it to honor what appears as Principle. **Principle is invisible but the effect is certainly felt!** When you are Principle in expression in the midst of the intellectual realm of to-day, "they" do not know what to do with it, because it is the offering force in any office either it would not be termed "universal in its adaptations"! *And you think you have alternatives?!* Does a grape in seed form have an alternative to become an apple? Does the seed of Love have an alternative to become other than Love? Does Man, the seed divine, have an alternative to be other than Man? That is termed "God-Man." Why is it termed God-Man? Because it is the generic term for allness.

What you consider balance is the antithesis of what balance is! Who ever heard of a plus and a minus balancing? Ask your accountants! But is this not what we base our lives upon? A plus and a minus. A positive and a negative cancel each other out, and we have a state that we all can detect if we are aware. It is the state that is termed "passive."

The passive state is the result of the positive and negative attempting to bring satisfaction. It is impossible! If it were possible, there would have been a negative God and a positive God; the divine would have been a positive man and a negative woman, or a negative man and a positive woman. You see how quickly we get to the point of saying, "It is the power of a woman behind every successful man .. for he is negative!" Even a president is said to have been a successful president because of the positive woman behind him! Who is *ahead* of him? *The divine Principle that has been forgotten due to the passive acceptance of the divided sense as acceptable and profitable and successful!* These are all transitory, all ephemeral, and what can be the verdict? "Well done, thou good and faithful servant"? "Inherit the kingdom of God and all that is prepared for you"? Impossible! Stay in after school! Go back to Earth and do it over again until your work is more than a recitation, until you *experience* the transformative power of a divine intention!

What do you have in your experience that points to your ability to experience a divine intention? The awareness that you are passing and that *I AM the Light to that passing*. If you can say, "I can see 'me' passing," then you know that I AM not in the passing, and your "me" is a suffering for it to be so now until *I come* and restore all things unto the kingdom.

You are dealing with an incredible force-field because you are dealing with the force that is capable of re-ordering your computer and having you mentally programmed to enunciate your own divinity and appear to be able to face your "me." If you can successfully program your computer to live a lie (which you have done all these years), then you can successfully program the computer to experience the divine Law of Balance, experience the divine fulcrum, and know in this there is active the divine Law of Compensation.

When the heart is *right*, the head cannot be *left*, for it appears as the foremost piece on your trunk to reach to the heavens and to receive the electrical force-field so that your tongue may dictate the electrical heartstrings' message, strung to the seven strings all tuned to the pitch, "I love wondrous Light!"

What are you doing these days? Gadding or God-ing? Begging or bowing? How do you exemplify involuntarily the spontaneous presence of an awareness that has the clear intention marked upon your forehead? The personality veils the Path, but the veil was rent when man was to enter the temple of his own glory. **What is that temple of his own glory? That structure that bears into time the wonders of the weightless, conditionless State of being Real!**

The old song "What Is My Task?" can only be asked of one who is wavering or has forgotten that the purpose of birth is to ask "Is it Real?" The purpose of death must have birth as an attendant either it could never appear to pass beyond your limited range of vision.

> **Death is that state of living that the limited sight cannot see, for it bears no resemblance to your capsule of limitation!**

This is why it is wonderful now, as an abstract exercise, to try to practice every day knowing what IS true in the avenues where others have forgotten that Truth is marching in the rhythmic intention, and a divine awareness walks in a blazing countenance called you. Your countenance should bear radiance and fragrance, not the stale breath of a dying branch or the sad, crumpled leaves of one who has forgotten the Source of wonder.

All Words are used as a means of holding your attention, for by holding your attention, you have been freed from the aging process of the mind. This is why study is so important because the more you study the Real, the less you have the aging effect of the unreal. If you think you are an intelligence utilizing the divine, then you will age anyway!

The divine appearing as intelligence utilized appears as a transcendental etude. Liszt was not the only one who had it up his sleeve! It was a *tour de force*, for sure, but what a joy to have found that *Man is a Song!* In that, the harmonic basis can be utilized, orchestrated for what is deemed the requirements of a setting given to a man and his script for the composition that allows one to see that the pitch of Reality is the open door to receiving the beneficence of the divine.

What a diapason of Sound, for when you accept it and are it, then you will realize that all the words have only been used up to the point where you can say, "My God, all those words, all those lectures, and now that the mind is still, the Silence has never been broken! It was the noise of my own mind that appeared as the words from another's mouth while he sat in silence before the wonder of God-Being."

I so enjoy this octave and the interval expressed as this Transmission. May you find it a dominant feature in the days that you will awaken unto. *What is a day in the serial of time when the Lord God omnipotent hath made it irradiant, One, divine?!*

The way of Passion! I would like to see a passive have passion! It is the fire that melts ice; it is even warmth that melts it. You do not have to be near the flame; the secondary characteristic of it is the heat. Dance in the Center of it if you dare!

▼

It is obvious that the picture is changing and therefore it cannot be Real, for the test of Reality is its unchanging Nature.

Chapter XVI

The Woo of God

ego

language

perception

new millennium

Invisible

Source

The Woo of God

There are some poems that I opened up to by Rumi:

What Jesus Runs Away From[1]

The son of Mary, Jesus, hurries up a slope
    as though a wild animal were chasing him.
Someone following him asks, "Where are you going?
    No one is after you." Jesus keeps on,
saying nothing, across two more fields. "Are you
    the one who says words over a dead person,
so that he wakes up?" *I am.* "Did you not make
    the clay birds fly?" *Yes.* "Who then
could possibly cause you to run like this?"
    Jesus slows his pace.

I say the Great Name over the deaf and the blind,
    they are healed. Over a stony mountainside,
and it tears its mantle down to the navel.
    Over non-existence, it comes into existence.
But when I speak lovingly for hours, for days,

---

1. *The Essential Rumi*, translation by Coleman Barks with John Moyne (San Francisco: Harper San Francisco, 1995), p. 204.

with those who take human warmth
and mock it, when I say the Name to them, nothing
   happens. They remain rock, or turn to sand,
where no plants can grow. Other diseases are ways
   for mercy to enter, but this non-responding
breeds violence and coldness toward God.
   I am fleeing from that.

As little by little air steals water, so praise
   dries up and evaporates with foolish people
who refuse to change. Like cold stone you sit on
   a cynic steals body heat. He doesn't feel
the sun. Jesus wasn't running from actual people.
   He was teaching in a new way.

How a Sheikh Is with a Community[2]

Here is how a sheikh is with a community:
when you're inside the presence of a true human being,
it's like being on Noah's ark.

Muhammed said, "I am an ark in the flood
of time. You are the ones I'm carrying."

Even if asleep, you're still on board!
Don't try to survive without a teacher.

Sometimes your sheikh will be angry, sometimes kind.
Any attention is the same attention.

Sometimes he makes you green and quiet like the ground
in Spring, sometimes puffed up and arrogantly loud.

Sometimes he gives you dull, clay-like qualities,
so that roses and eglantine can grow,
flowers only the Friend sees.

Empty out your disbelief.
The transformation that's coming

---

2. *Say I am you: Poetry Interspersed with Stories of Rumi and Shams*, translated by
   John Moyne and Coleman Barks (Athens, Georgia: Maypop, 1994), pp. 84-85.

will not be like a human being visiting
the moon, but more like the way sugarcane
becomes sugar. Not so much like
water vaporizing, more like

an embryo having its first rational thought.
Ride the horse of *fana,* and let it
change to Boraq!

Keep your soul moving toward its Friend.
No hands or feet are required for the going.

Just embark on this boat
and stay on it!

Many blessings from the unseen shower down
on the sheikh, as they do here on Husam!

When you give, gifts are given you,
a thousandfold. Inorganic matter
turns to visionary eloquence.

When you're generous with your love,
you're really loving yourself,
because what comes back is so amazing.

▼ ▼ ▼

Richard H.) Mr. Mills, what brought you to
the statement that "I and my Father *is* One"?

A conflict which arose when I was quite young. I heard
the minister say in church, "I and my Father are One." Then
I heard what sinners we were and what spiritual vagabonds
we were — and it did not make sense. When my Sunday
School classmates reached twelve, they were all baptized,
but I refused, to the consternation of everyone including
Mom and Dad. I would not. When I was twenty-one, I was

baptized. I said, "I will be baptized to satisfy you because it is all right now."

It was at that time that I started considering the contradictory statements. If I and my Father are inseparable, the only way we can be inseparable is to have the *Source* and the *evidence of the Source* inseparable. *If the Father is the Source, then the evidence must be the activity commensurate unto the Father. This is the power to restore "all things" to their rightful place in order for them to be freed from the limitations that symbology has placed upon them.* The first and foremost among those symbols are the forms termed "Adam and Eve." No wonder we all looked at the apple and turned it golden, for it is a very important key, as they say, to Paradise.

At this underlined, special time in the century, perhaps you have perceived that the question about the birthing of the next millennium is one of great concern. It is strange that the millennium is being considered with such extravagant concern (without knowing what to be extravagant over!). No other year seems to be of concern to people, and yet there are 365 rungs to the ladder of each year. No one says what is the cause of the concern. No one asks, "Why should we be concerned?" or "Why should we not be concerned?" It is obvious that concern is not in the forefront of anyone's considerations, any more than is the *content* of what constitutes the forthcoming peregrination through time.

People say that the world seems to long for something. The world does not long for anything! You cannot say that the stage is responsible if you forget your lines. The world is at rest, and those of you who are concerned about *it* are attempting to evade your own state.

> **You will not experience the world other than the way you appear to *perceive* it, and by what you bear in the realm of the attainment of perception.**

Ellen M.) N. M. said, "Your Work has directly to do with a necessary shift in perspective
and perception — for the new millennium."

She pointed out that the *perception* is essential and the
perspective is essential. You will have neither from the
standpoint of being only an intellectual summation of agreeing thought-forms about what is wrong with your world.
Leave the world alone; it does not owe you a thing! All you
can do is appreciate its form for allowing *you* to have one.
Upon *its* stage you could be identified.

In listening to people concerned about the state of
human-kind, even the practitioners in psychology are finding little permanent resolution in the avenues for lessening
conflict within the intellect. Some feel that words used in the
ordinary way to convey a feeling and a meaning, and words
used to delineate the Invisible under the Rod of correct
usage are the same. They are not! They cannot be. The
words that go with the thought-patterns of the intellect refer
to the camaraderie that exists with thought-forms. The
thought-forms that are re-awakened under the Rod of correct usage in the Light of the Invisible, force one to escape
from the common usage of words, because the common
usage of words weaves a garment of contentment when
there is no *content*.

We have an enormous quantity of words, believe it or
not! The language is filled with words which hardly anyone
uses. In our ordinary conversation we have dropped from
the average usage of twenty-five thousand words to a very
few thousand. Even a schooled language for a specialized
course dealing with an intellectual complaint does not
relieve the complainer, for the complainer and the complaint
are manufactured and sustained in the same *groove* of mentality! The groove just needs to be a bit wider, and it is the
grave! The only difference between "groove" and "grave" is
the *a* and the *oo!*

It is one thing to be *groovy,* which means you are in tune with all others in a rut, but you shake it out and shake it down and hoe it down with your common folk wee-talk! Few understand the importance of being a fiddler on the roof and the importance of being a virtuoso in intellectual attainment, beyond being a virtuoso on the instrument. "When you have once gone to the roof of the house, do not go back into it to take anything out!" I wonder if the fiddler knows enough not to go back into the house to take anything out. In other words, *you cannot drag into your future what you have left behind, in order to give you a zone of contentment, when it has lost content.*

There is such a vast usage of specialized language. Books are written in order to make instruments intelligent and the operators ignorant! What is in operation in your diction, quality or quantity? Remember, a loose tongue is like a cannon.

If the Word of God is one with God (and it is), how can you consider a teaching to be of significance if it holds you in the system of belief that attempts to tell you that sin exists in the vocabulary of God? Sin is not a quality commensurate with the Source; sin is what is dreamt when the Spirit and the Word have lost the power of diction. *The Spirit and the Word seem to lose the power of diction when the source of inspiration is an intellectual argument, or augmentation of disagreement, or adjudication, instead of the utilization of wisdom and the offering of freedom from a system of diction that has created a belief of fear.*

Why do you compress yourself via the modes of mentality and via the behavior of the modes intoned? You do not have to pay any mind to what is not True. Why do you spend so much time climbing the ladder of each year, still finding that a baby in diapers is worshipped so you can start over, changing your own mental diapers over again. No wonder . . exists in Times Square. "Times squared" does nothing but offer the confines of a walled civilization terrified of the unknown, and the energy that could elevate, enhance, and prosper is dwarfed into the ballooned considerations of inflated egos. Without agreement among many, how do they know they have any existence at all?!

What is an ego but the outcome of a wrong utilization of words of description? An "ego" is a name that is given to describe the unknown Soul of you with a gown of "you" that has no awareness of "you." The Soul is not known by *"you,"* and yet, through worldly ignorance, we all agree that ego surrounds us and each of us has one. It is so "generous" of the common consent to allow each to have an ego. It is true communism: Each one seems to have an ego, and there is no reluctance to evidence it! It is just the varying degrees of size.

The Soul of you, the id of you, the unknown part of you, is really waiting to be discovered. *It is not lost!* The Reality of What IS is not lost because of "you." It is because of you that the language is fortified with power that restricts the usage of Force, in the diction unbecoming to the elevation of the invisible Host. Your invisible Host is the sought-after comforter of your Being, for the comforter of your Being fortifies you with the strength of conviction, and that conviction arises as a result of attempting to appropriate it unto yourself. Why would you appropriate it unto yourself? You have to accept something.

> **How do you know the Invisible IS? It allows what *is not* to be identified, and in its grace, "it" still *seems* to be!**

That is the wonder of God-Being: the dual aspect, appearing as a result of the invisible appropriation of the divine as a living, vibrant experience, postulating the position man must take in order to give benediction and cause the multitude to melt in the crystallized thought-forms of limitation!

Tonality breaks the crystal that has inclusions. Every crystal of intellectual attainment has inclusions, and if it is thought personal, it cannot help but be shattered. Sooner or later, your intellectual demise is inevitable! (What a glorious future!)

The Mind of God may only be that force that wipes the suggestion of chaos from your evolutionary scale of attainment and allows you to perceive what is precipitated upon the attainment of a higher octave. Thus, you have the distance to view your Earth and the activity as a scene animated by the motifs that bear the Light/Leit force of operatic content.

> Man is a Song and he was made to sing,
> Not about the counting house and not about
>   the King of Kings.
> He was given an anthem, and it was given to
>   praise,
> For in the dual considerations of his day life,
> He had to see and feel how the triad of
>   glory sounded when raised!

Concord dwarfs time spent in movement and bestows freshness. Dissonance is protracted pain. The reason people love dissonance is because dissonance experienced starts to become a pleasurable evidence of your "living," for it bears not the fructifying radiation of Presence! Dissonance waits to be *resolved*. In music, we can resolve a dissonance and bring about an end or we can bring about a suggestion of an end, and find it deceptive.

You cannot take your own life and get away with it! Some return from the grave and tell of after-death experiences. You cannot take your life if it is not to go, and why hold it if it *is* to go?

Which one of the countless "yous" are you watching? You have so many! Since "you" watch what appears as me, **why do you superimpose upon your vision what is only**

relevant unto "you"? Why do you not cease being a visionary, allow the impostor within you to be posited as an offering to attainment, and walk free from the belief of having to worship an unknown Source or God? It was said, centuries ago, "God whom you *ignorantly* worship, Him declare I unto you." How is it possible to use this language if it does not point to something beyond it? Why would you worship a God in ignorance? What does "ignorance" mean? Lacking what is essential to resolve **dissonance.**

What must you know about dissonance? It has to be resolved; it is crying out to be resolved. It is the modern-day voice crying in the wilderness, *"Prepare ye the way of harmonic progression from sense to Soul. Enter into the Pitch of a universal activity, found only when you pass from contentment with what isn't into the infinite possibilities of agitating with Light the very fabric of thought that is grayed and dulled by centuries of belief."*

You are told that you are on the edge of a new millennium. What does that really mean? What will the celebrations be when it seems to happen? It is going to have to be one costly dream — the fireworks will be spectacular! I wonder if balloons inflated with egos will be floating around! I wonder if the fireworks exploding will fill you with amazement. In your compressed state, you do not realize that the Fire *does* work. The only thing you have to know is the fuse, which is the Father's use of the Self energized. The fuse has to be ignited with wonder and become the very spark that causes another to take fire. What does fire tell you? Take too long and you may be a cinder! Perceive what it is, and translate.

What does compression do? In the editing of recordings, *compression is used on the highs and the lows so that they will be contained within the parameter of limitation of the object recording an experience of tonality.* If tonality has to be compressed because the vehicle cannot take it and give back authenticity, **why would you wish to compress the tonality of Truth by the parameters of belief?!**

Why do you allow the cast to fall down before false language? Why do you not stand in the volition of knowing what it is to be the *Father's use?* Why do you not perceive that after the Amazons had their day, then there might have been the Matriarch, but now, if we put the Patriarch and the Matriarch together, we have an arc, and it is this arc that may hold a great promise. The arc is a covenant that was made with the harmonic state and the dissonant state, and it was to be an eternal promise for those who were always looking, always hearing and listening, for what was heard as a Tone of significance. That bore a spectrum of interiorized responsiveness, and that is the quality that is being reawakened in *you,* **because you can no longer be as you seem to be!** You are truly a tonality of significance when you are not content with any type of pitch. Do not pitch any kind of woo; ask why.

Remember the finger pointing to the moon. Do not mistake it. What is the point of going to the moon? It is said to be so outside yourself. If it is costly to go to the moon that is so far outside yourself (and it has cost billions of dollars), can you imagine how cheap it is to find the center of the universe?! It does not cost a penny, for it was the gift of the Light. It was stated, "All is thine." Whose? **If All that *I* have is yours, does it mean something is withheld?**

Why do you behave as if you are people filled with a legitimate beef about the legality of your Inheritance?! Why do you get so "beefed-up" with complaint and moods and vacillation? No wonder the people who walk this plane are so overweight. They are *under* weight, and the mind alleviates it in order to have contentment. From what? They are under weight but since they do not have an energized conscience, they consider themselves "overweight" like so many others. They are under the weight, and *there is no greater weight than knowing you have not fought a good fight for the Light*. What is the Light? That which allows you to understand the wooing of the Source, and no need of why.

We were not born to question; we were born to respond to Love! We were given to Love, and you goddamn it by fractionalizing your divine force and discriminating it in the likes of "you" and "me" and the family tree and different colors of race and creed. *There is but one divine attraction, and that is the Woo of God! God's Wooing beckons you to be unbound from the shackles of intellectual specialization which, through the subtle use of language, conceals your self-inflicted bondage. You could escape not only without you but within you, and find the content the miraculous gift of grace. Amazing! And you say, "The fireworks were amazing!"*

The work of the Fire is amazing! Do not allow the water of your unconscious and ungrateful state to attempt to put it out! It never can, for the Fire is so great that it meets the water face to face, and it turns to steam. You think the Fire is out? It has caused a *translation* of that which would destroy it! That which would destroy it has become harmless steam which now ascends and condenses as clouds, to be precipitated once again for another round, a return to the petals of time. Isn't it remarkable that we have the rainbow as the arc of a comfort, and the rainbow in a dew drop?

If you see your stalk starting to bud, look for the dew/do, for it will be the evidence that you have the conviction and you have the courage to allow your appearance in time to reveal your fragrant Nature, and your petals those facets of accomplishment that bear, even in the ashes, the inevitable essence of the fragrant state of Being. Always look to your rose and see Eros if you wish, but remember, "you" cannot deaden the Fire of your experience because of the fear of your Identity not being human. *You are afraid to BE Real. Do you dare to be Real?* It means that you cannot allow what *is not* to be responded unto as if *it* is!

> Listen with patience and know in might
> That the point of a needle bears no groove
> in Light.

It pierces asunder a compression, a state,
And erases the grave as a hidden fate.
The Fates are watching and they are
        clapping their hands,
For in the recognition of Wonder, the rod of
        Light conducts I AM!

Acting, doing, being! Wear your gown of a human and bear the *hue* commensurate to the cosmic blossoms of a celestial garden. Do not be afraid of color! Develop a force-field capable of wearing it, and then perhaps the Mantle will be found on your shoulders and someone will be grabbing the hem of your garment. Then you can say, "Goodness has gone from me"? No! You might say, *"Love has cognized Love!"* In this be content!

▼

To Be is not to set the world on fire; to
Be is to be so fired that the world
seems to be changed!

Chapter XVII

Do You See as I See?

choice

belief

simplicity

conception

sword of Truth

undivided State

Love

Do You See as I See?

We are gathered together to celebrate what has been a pageant of the mind with the birth of a Redeemer. We are gathered together in the festive knowingness that the possibilities of Being born immaculately are ever at hand, and if it were not for an Example in a play of such proportions and such drama, we could never be able to entertain such a probability of self-exculpation.

We are now perceiving as never before that the dream of this great birth of a Savior who is Christ the Lord is none other than the symbolic need to arrange matter in a stable place and allow ourselves to feed it the straw of the mind and leap beyond the quiescent dormancy commensurate with the sleeping state of the animal.

We are asked to believe that a Savior was born and was cognized by the Wise Men. This is perfectly true, because *it does take a wise man to adore That which is not perceived other than in the symbolic sense as a figure.* You *see,* and yet you do not believe, and yet believing, you see *not.* Where you look may not be into that area where there is verification, if you are allowing the mind to be transported to that state that is termed one still imbued with the intellectual mythology surrounding the erudition of a religious scenario.

All religion has been based upon the need for people to worship the unknown Self of their own making, and yet, man would not have worshiped something termed "God" if within himself the State had not already been waiting for acceptance! We never seek what is without our own comprehension; it only appears to be without our *willingness* to accept its presence.

We have been taught that we should understand before accepting, and it has always been pointed out that understanding is what another says about a situation *after* he has experienced it!

To experience an immaculate conception is possible for every man and woman, for you are a structure of the Temple made not with hands; you are the Temple itself, but you cannot be that experience if you structure your experience upon the visual and the sentient.

> **You must understand that to be Real one does not need to forfeit anything other than his present state that would cause him to be bound to the transient.**
>
> **It does not take time to think right!**

On this plane of choice it is so much "fun" (people like to create problems!) to suffer the irritation and the restlessness and the uneasiness that comes with thinking you have a choice. You have not! You were only given an opportunity to test your ability to move with the higher promptings of your inner Self in the face of the contrasting differences, a result of choice.

Differences are of no consequence whatsoever; they are the spice to the experience. However, they appear to be the *strife* to our experience, and the time is rife with changes to take place.

People are saying that a new age is upon us; that is because the present is not Now! *The future is dreamed because the past is so prevalent in our considerations.* It was also pointed out by a guest at dinner that it is impossible to use the word in Hebrew for "I am" because it is "Jehovah" and that is the holy name of God, and you cannot take it in vain. *You have to say "I was," and thus the past has a force of holding you to a condition that only can exist if you refuse to live in the Now!*

It has always been said that to live in the Now is to be present with the wonder of Being and allow what *is not* to parade in order to satisfy those who believe in the transient until *I come.* "I come suddenly!" You are not programmed to believe this. If you were, you would stop dating with "Yuma dates"! When you have too many dates with "you," you undoubtedly have to find a pit sooner or later. This pit is so filled with other seedlings-of-belief that it takes a long time for a palm to bear fruit and not bear the dust of the desert of belief.

Your arrangement is so fortuitous because you have seeded yourselves in such a way as to be adapted to the radiance of unlimited possibilities by being present with the wonder of radiance. The radiance of infinite possibilities is cast upon us all, for we are not custodians of the world; we are here only to be what IS. Many have asked what is going to happen to the world in the future, but that is presupposing you cannot say "I AM." Your future will be none other than the past dressed-up unless I AM present, and in that case, what is a new year but a suggestion that I *was?*

Time and space are nothing but the attempt of a form to explain itself on the face of time, but the face of time ages; that is why you watch. Then you look upon it and see how the hands move, and you say, "Ah, the numbers mark the passing hours." Then that little hand tells you the seconds that make up your minutes and your minutes that make up your hours. Suddenly you are looking at a face of time to tell you that it is passing instead of realizing that **the watch reveals the Nowness of the present. The time is just for those who believe in a sequence of holy events.**

Time has no aging presence when there is a sequence of holy events, and a holy event is like that which is termed the birth of a Savior, the birth of a Jesus, or the birth of a wonder Child. Time has nothing to do with wonder. That is why wonder is such a marvel.

> **Wonder allows you to be now won/One!**
> **When man sees wonder as timeless,**
> **the timeless is experienced as Presence which**
> **bears its own verification.**

The Truth cannot be verified other than through the irritation of a lie. The honesty of Truth is always the irritation to the partial honesty of a lie. You can always tell, when Truth is marching, rhythm is certainly part of the inherent nature.

For a Savior to have been born unto the world, it must have meant through the prophetic nature of the past that everyone was to expect a deliverance from the mortal conditions of that time, as we are expecting a change in this time. *What is "this time" other than That time all dressed-up for a ball? Why a ball? Because everyone will appear to rock and roll with the rhythm that is heard, but seldom do they ever attune to the unheard rhythm of their own Being, which beats in rapture with the little drummer boy's gift to the Child.*

Remember, *the drum points to the unrelenting, rhythmic beat of intention,* and the reason Mary smiled is because through her rhythm and her acceptance of rhythm, a Child was born as Presence. Others cognizing it gave Presence presents. *If recognition is not present, presence cannot bear Presence.* That is why it seems that ashrams, holy communities, are formed, because presence bears Presence presents.

Without that Presence there is always need for verification. What is the verification? *Constancy.* If you are not a constant, you do not know, for the life of you, how to give a constant pitch of universal significance. You cannot attune to your own frequency, for "you" really do not have one. *The frequency that is Real is one that is attuned to the fact that "I and my Father is One now, and not shall be." As soon as you start using your tenses in such a way as to relieve yourself of tension, then you find the whole way is paved with excuses and procrastination.*

> **Procrastination is the very onset
> of the deterioration of the will.**

As long as you procrastinate you are refusing the instantaneity of Being, a possible experience.

> **That instantaneity of Being is a spontaneous
> act of Nowness in spite of the protracted
> sense of progress from sense to Soul.**

The Child born in a manger suggests the time element of birth, growth, maturity, and decay, but to be born anew does not mean you have to die and come back and cause a traffic jam! It means that you should be born anew by accepting a new birth certificate, and **that new birth certificate tells you that you are not a mind-being but you are Conscious-Being, and being conscious, declare it as "I AM."**

"I am being conscious" is only a suffering for the moment, because I AM is the Power that allows the suggestion of Presence to suffer this interlude of a dimensional experience for a brief time only! Why? Because the mind is conjectured to be on the face of time and, as soon as anything is timed, it is limited. As soon as anything is named, it is walled, and as soon as anything is known intellectually, it is thought into impotency.

That which IS is not an intellectual attainment; That which IS allows the intellect to appear to have attained!

You see, we do not want to think we are all One. We do not want to consider that we are all part and parcel of one glorious, undivided State. We want to think we are all separate so we can have our own separate lives and our own separate lies and our own separate agenda in the realm of chaos due to the belief system of choice. "Choose ye this day whom ye will serve, God or mammon." God, the One altogether lovely, or mammon, the divided state!

The divided state is "the opposition"; it is "the other party" which has such an incredible voting system in today's world. It has the speakers who tell you, "Through process you are going to achieve this. Come hell or high water, you are going to achieve this." *The One Party says, "I AM All and there is no party other than all that I AM." That is such a destroyer of fun because you take on the incredible artistry of Being, which means that you develop such a dexterity in your thought, in your word, and in your deed that you can appear to be just like anyone else while you remain as you really are.* But what do you do?

Everyone asks what everyone *does,* in this country. It was pointed out to me in France that everyone in America asks what everyone does and then decides how to treat him. In France, everyone speaks without ever asking what another does, for if you are listening correctly, even a "yes" or a "no" will reveal their openness or closed-ness. **Remember, just because you know what people do, does not mean that they "do." You only do what comes naturally when there is only the natural present.**

So many people try to make-it sharp and they cannot stand it, so others come along and try to make-it flat. The Tonality is the same, because there we have the enharmonic key! **There we have the enharmonic key in an intellectual concept of the coincidence of the human and the divine.** It is an enharmonic state. On one side you can see me and I say "I AM"; on another side I say "I AM," which you cannot see but you know me and that is natural. Whether or not you accept the verity of an enharmonic state is entirely up to you, for I have no options. *I took a chance and defied my "thought" intention, to the astonishment of associates.*

Before I agreed to speak if asked, I had a small group of so-called friends which numbered about three hundred. I sent three hundred Christmas cards every year and wrote and signed them. As soon as I agreed to speak, it dropped to six! You are here, so you save postage!

What is the post-age? Is it not costly?! It is the suggested distance that has to be covered in order for a message to be heard, and frequently it is inscribed. But what if the present age is instantaneous cognition of the message that I AM All?! *Why procrastinate and fill the pockets of belief with the five-cent/sense world of options?*

Today people seem to be schooled in polemics in order to evade meeting the challenge of the Sword. The Sword of Truth is so sharp when a true state is delivered; the Sword delivers one blow and reveals the correct facet, and if there is an inclusion within that building stone of your so-called Temple, it will be revealed.

> **You can always test the validity of your**
> **belief system by your agility to leap out of it.**

A belief system is only there for you as an excuse until *I* come.

That is a revelation which comes from the manger; it does not come from growth, maturity, and decay. It comes from the manger of simplicity. Jesus said that you were supposed to become as little children. *Such as these, come unto Me and inherit the Kingdom.* That is the idea of being birthed. I mean, you look so big. *I do not expect you to "rewomb" it and do it again!* John was love, and **Love does not need to be rewombed; it needs to be reloomed so that it becomes the essence of the thread through the maze of time.**

> *Everyone who bears the mark of the divine bears Love, for it is emblazoned upon the escutcheon of your achievement if you have achieved a transcendence over the mind of limitation.*

That thread is essential for your to-morrows for you to be able to walk among all types of men and women and realize that they think they are types, and you have already got the set! That is how you can know your next book may be unnamed and unnumbered, but it will bear the preface that posts an age and bans the suggestion of the need of opposites and demands the balanced state or the androgyne.

The future demands a withdrawal from the belief that opposites balance. It demands the cognition that every man and every woman bears, *within,* the ability of the balanced state, if he will transcend the belief system which accompanies his physicality. *You cannot expect peace when your own inner country is divided by the power of suggestion. Your power of suggestion suggests that you are "this." The birth says, "No, no, no, no. In the manger of simplicity, I AM only known as Light."* It is when you are named that you may become a Savior; when you are Light, you are so to the world. This is how, through the enhancement of Identity, Jesus accomplished. When He was telling the priests off in the Temple, He was interrupted and was told, "Your mother and your father seek ye sorrowingly." He said, "Who is my mother? Who is my father? Don't disturb me; I am about the Father's business (Perhaps He could have added:) of Being motherless and fatherless from the standpoint of Truth. I have been born in the naturalness of simplicity."

As long as you are bred and cultured in your limited tradition, you have to work so hard to break the bonds that have bound you to an intellectual symmetry of thought that seems to bear logic. It is in this very realm of logic where we become sedated, because that is where all who have an incredible realm of logic live, in the realm of *nous*.[1] As soon as doubt enters the logic, fear arises and then develops paranoia! Then the whole belief system creates *metanoia!* You can delineate it and speak about it in the most lucid way, but let me tell you, we know without a doubt (and those who doubt know *with* doubts) that when *nous*/new is old and no paramount news is available, annoyance sets in, and what was above (metanoia), which could have made complete, is ignored. And the next degree is what? The lower kingdoms. You have structured those because you have refused to claim "I AM." You cannot structure such a state if you say and live as "I am."

Do you know that every problem in the world rests in one area? No one will say "I AM" and effect change. They effect change by offering their credentials. If people are coming before you for work, for a new position, you ask them for their credentials because without their credentials you cannot perceive where the credibility lies. (Lies!) You can see what they have attained, but if they are wrapped-up in trying to make unity work in disunity, they might as well try to make the world a better place by being in the world. They are in it, but they may think they are out of it. They are not!

If this evening is being experienced by you and me, if you go within yourselves (whatever that is!) and take your

---

1. From the Greek word meaning "reason" or "intellect," used here to refer to the common level of everyday thinking.

thought off me, I do not exist, this room does not exist, no one in this room exists. But if you focus again on me, then we all appear to exist and experience this evening. It is interesting. There must be one State common to each and every one that, if cognized, would work in such unity that we could take the world right into our hands. That is how it is taken into your hand. In the cognition of where your attention is, there AM I also, and where your attention is not, there is your world in chaos.

You do not bother trying to change your world! Do not belong to a political party! Just be aware of the opposition, because it would try to have you divided in your ranks. The opposition always purports the wonder of process and power. The Truth is the exact opposite. *"My peace I give unto you. Not as the world giveth give I unto you."*[2] That is the Point!

Remember, what you adore is not the baby in the manger, it is the birth of a new idea within yourself that is immaculately conceived because it has been seeded by your divine intention to be Real.

Feed your night-mare with your mattress (hay!), but stall the oppressor by disrobing him of his suggested power of polemics inaugurated into your stream of conviction.

The Wise Men are wise because they still adore. Are you a wise man or a wise woman? If you do not adore, you will never find the way to go home! You will say, "I'm tired and I want to go to bed. I had a little drink about an hour ago, and it went right to my head!" Where do you think it all is? Upstairs?! It is not even upstairs! That is why you do not need an anesthetic to have your brain operated upon; it is senseless! Upon your death it is taken out with straws through your nostrils. It is wonderful to be so well-educated!

As I was saying at dinner, if you entered an atomic press and had all the holes squeezed out of you, what would be

---

2. John 14:27.

left could be seen on the head of a pin! I wonder what type of argument can be elicited from one speck of dust to another, even though they are on a common pin!

There is one Point, and you are stuck with it in spite of your deadpan physiognomy! As I once said to an audience, "Remember, your faces are not porcelain-ized!" There is always a tail when a tuck is taken. You can see when you take a stand against a tale, tucks are always taken because a garment always changes in size. Your mental garment always has to change when the true Tale is told.

It may be that Mary and Joseph both knew that what could be born beyond the womb of suggestion was a Child that would be uncontaminated and unfettered by the obstetrics of time and the physiological empire of suggestion.

Remember that when conception takes place, it is believed to be a journey into an unknown land where the voyageur takes the beach and meets a new beginning within the darkness of the womb. Remember, that is all conjured because everyone believes it. It shows you the magical power of believing the same act.

Everyone has thought in the terms of acquiescing to the acceptance of difference as part of the spectrum of newness. It is not difference that makes newness. What makes newness is the natural, freed from the contamination of a belief system. That is what is new!

A Natural-Man is not going to be concerned about an unnatural one, and a Natural-Man is not going to be concerned about a sharp one or a flat one! I just told you about the faces that were porcelainized, the flat ones, and I have just told you to-night about the sharp ones. The Natural-Man perceives what a birth is, and it is not out of the womb; it is *before* entering the belief system of personal, creative acts.

If you can be born without the belief system of time (*without:* not here but out there), then you can be born beyond the face of limitations. You only bear a face for others to cognize you and a name so that your face can be called.

If I did not take on a form like you, you could not call me K. G., and I had to be in order for the mill to get moving! One person once said to me, "Beloved Son of the Light, remember, the wheels of the mills grind slowly but grind exceedingly small. Have patience, beloved Son." I said, "I have nothing to do with *that* mill, nothing whatsoever to do with it! I am not going to grind anything." What a way to okay slowness . . or speed! I do not believe in any of those drugs! No wonder you have a drug system, you breed it within your attitudes: speed and slowness, uppers and downers; naturals, sharps, flats; ups and downs. That is not the way to modulate from sense to Soul!

You cannot modulate if you are intoxicated with possibilities. You can only modulate by knowing what type of robe you wear. It was once said, "Take My robe upon you and think of Me." And I said, "Take the robe of *Unfoldment*™ upon you and be as I AM." Then, for those who perceive you, you will manifest what they deem necessary as your robe. It may be the art of writing, it may be the art of speaking, it may be the art of music, it may be the art of painting. Others will see you in the role that is devoid of the barbs of limitation surrounding egocentricity.

All I am really saying is, be natural by being Real, and let those who want to be sharp be sharp, and let those who want to be flat be flat, because to a natural, they are only altered states of a suggestion. Being natural, I AM never altered but only appear at the altar in the service of Being altogether lovely in the service of the One. That is all there IS.

You are Love, honesty, Truth, manifested with integrity at the core of your hub; thus you can be a cog in the wheel of suggestion and stop the eternal cycle of reincarnations, which do what? Jam the whole system! The world has become intoxicated with having choices. *It is not drunken with wine; it is drunken with choice.* It is this drunkenness with choice that the Teachers (and many present but unseen) are worried about because it is blocking the natural flow that is relevant unto those who wish to experience and *have to* experience choice. They say this is the only planet on which you can experience choice.

> I did not come to teach you anything;
> I came to take your attention and
> show you how your attention is what you
> bear upon the authentic Nature that is
> termed "the ground of your very Being."
> It is never in person, it is never in process,
> and it is forever blooming, for it always
> bears the flowering of its nature.

If you are Love, as you are, you cannot help but evidence its meaningful Presence, which does what? Alter/altar! You have to be able to move, with the dexterity becoming an artist, from octave to octave without "thumbing" it! *You cannot superimpose another's experience upon yourself as if it were yours.* The tail/tale is this: Frequently it drags in the dust because you weigh it down with your "mud-like" presence instead of your Light attention.

How are you going to change the gravitational pull of Earth if you do not counter it with the buoyancy of being Real?! Do you ever stop and consider that you take on this framework of separateness in order to experience separateness via a form with a sensorial apparatus that allows you to sense your projection called "others"? There is no such thing as "falling in love" with another. If you fall in love with anyone, it should be the Self and then it might appear as another. But you cannot fall in love with somebody else if you cannot love your Self.

The reason marriages are rather strange to-day is because the people engaging in them may not have realized what is the Real, what is the natural State, before entering them. They may have been pretty sharp, you know, "the yuppies," but look at the dead pledges, the mortgages, trying to keep up with the Joneses, the beach boys! All you do then is roll with stones, and what do they do? They come back!

I thought we said that the stone was to be used in the Temple, and the one that was rejected has become the head of the corner. Why a stone? A stone is really the density of a tone waiting to be freed from its state. *A stone is nothing but the vibration that exists and manifests as such because someone who was logical dropped into the mineral state by refusing to accept the enharmonic state of 'nous' and ascend to the 'metanoia,' to the state beyond, or to the metaphysical, philosophical discernment that allows man to perceive the path of the Uncontradictable!*

When man is redeemed, the infringement of the force-field commensurate with division ceases. That is the redemption. "Thy redemption draweth nigh," the moment you can perceive how the immaculate conception is the availability here and now of Being bearing the newness commensurate with the eternality of the nameless God I AM.

You cannot say the name I AM (Jehovah) and put it into sound. It can never be uttered in time, only pointed to by the name "Jehovah." *Jehovah! It was never in the name, anyway; it was in the tonality that men heard the Creator sounding and they mistook it as being contained in a name!* That mistaken identity has given us the density of matter, and what we cannot see through, we make dense.

> **That is why in the newness of Being we will perceive Man as a Song, transparent as the stone upon which he must stand.**

Transparent Man, transparent stone, reveals the temple of Beauty bearing witness in the manifested artistic achievement of all those who enter its precincts. They enter through the acceptance of the nowness of its immaculate nature, just by being willing to be wholly in the embrace of the magic of the white Light of the Christ, of the Brother Buddha, and of all those Saints and Sages who have ascended through the belief realm of suggestion — beyond our reach, beyond our comprehension, beyond our time? No! The nowness of Being erases a time sequence of limitation and reveals the past, the forgotten story, and the future — the past drunken with expectations and hung over the present, waiting for the nowness of Being to be cognized.

Remember . . and you have. What? I AM not "this" but That. That is the Suchness of Being and the invulnerability of it, and yet it is the verification that is deemed present even without a name!

> **By being willing, man is perceived as the undying magnet of Love that appears to be a constant, radiating force between all those who love and expect a new birth in a moment of renunciation when man can leap via the trampoline of dexterity into the lap of the Infinite.**

Do not find yourselves timed beings other than for the fun of this drama we are playing on this stage. *Cognize yourselves as the radiance commensurate with the effulgent Son of the balanced State which is essential. The balanced State is what I AM, what you are when you forget "you" are and know I AM.*

Why fret[3] unless you are playing the guitar? Find a difficult hand position more simply attained! It is a suffering it to be so. You know when you be "soh," you have to go to "doh," and when the dough is raised, Principle is praised and a new octave of Being awaits your perception of the

---

3. You may find the definition and root meaning of this word "fret" very revealing and surprising, as you will find with many of the words used in these Unfoldments.™

tonality surrounding the rarefied language of the pristine state of Man! The birth in the manger points to That, these words point to That, your presence points to That, and in that Point be stuck with the pin of rejoicing and find yourself uncomfortable with an incorrect identity and perfectly at ease with the Identity of being a natural One to play upon the keyboard of the lyre of seven strings, all strung to the tune of "I Love wondrous Light!"

> Remember, this plane is one of choice.
> Do you think you have any, other than
> to be Real?

▼

W hat is the world? A platform for those to witness a Light coincidence!

Also Available from
Sun-Scape Publications

Kenneth George Mills

Tyranny of Love
The Key: Identity
The Golden Nail
A Word Fitly Spoken
The New Land!
Given to Praise!

Poetry

Words of Adjustment
Embellishments
Anticipations
Surprises

Audiocassettes

The Tonal Garment of The Word
Coat of Many Colors (with EarthStage Actors)
Freedom Is Found
The Quickening Spirit of Radiance
Near to the Fire
The Seal of Approval
The Newness of the Unchanging
The Beauty Unfoldment

▼

Rolland G. Smith

Poetry

Quiet Musings

▼

Nurit Oren

Ancient Stories Living Today
Retrieved from the Riches of the Cache